Windows®
Server 2003
Pocket Administrator

Nelson Ruest
Danielle Ruest

McGraw-Hill/Osborne

New York   Chicago   San Francisco
Lisbon   London   Madrid   Mexico City   Milan
New Delhi   San Juan   Seoul   Singapore   Sydney   Toronto

The *McGraw·Hill* Companies

McGraw-Hill/Osborne
2100 Powell Street, 10ᵗʰ Floor
Emeryville, California 94608
U.S.A.

To arrange bulk purchase discounts for sales promotions, premiums, or fund-raisers, please contact **McGraw-Hill**/Osborne at the above address. For information on translations or book distributors outside the U.S.A., please see the International Contact Information page immediately following the index of this book.

Windows® Server 2003 Pocket Administrator

1234567890 DOC DOC 019876543

ISBN 0-07-222977-2

Publisher   Brandon A. Nordin
Vice President & Associate Publisher   Scott Rogers
Acquisitions Editor   Francis Kelly
Project Editor   Elizabeth Seymour
Acquisitions Coordinator   Jessica Wilson
Technical Editor   Rod Trent
Copy Editors   Dennis Weaver
Proofreader   Susan Carlson Greene
Indexer   Valerie Perry
Composition   Carie Abrew
Illustrators   Kathleen Edwards, Melinda Lytle, Michael Mueller
Series Design   Peter F. Hancik, Lucie Ericksen, Elizabeth Jang
Cover Series Design   Jeff Weeks

This book was composed with Corel VENTURA™ Publisher.

We dedicate this book to Marie-Andrée, friend, daughter, partner, and collaborator. Thank you for your valuable help. Every day, you manage to amaze us by going far beyond our expectations.

About the Authors

Danielle Ruest is a workflow architect and consultant focused on people and organizational issues for large IT deployment projects. During her twenty-two year career, she has led change management processes, developed and delivered training, and managed communications programs during process-implementation projects.

Nelson Ruest is an enterprise architect specializing in change management. During his twenty-two year career, he has served as a computer operator, network administrator, and director for IT consulting firms. He is a Microsoft Certified Systems Engineer and Microsoft Certified Trainer. Presently, he is a senior enterprise consultant whose purpose is to assist organizations to master the technologies they depend on.

Danielle Ruest and Nelson Ruest are also the authors of *Windows Server 2003: Best Practices for Enterprise Deployment* (McGraw-Hill/Osborne, 2003; www.Reso-Net.com/WindowsServer) as well as *Preparing for .NET Enterprise Technologies: People, PCs and Processes Interacting in a .NET World* (Addison-Wesley, 2001; www.Reso-Net.com/EMF). They are frequent contributors and product reviewers for .NET Magazine (www.thedotnetmag.com) and MCP Magazine (www.mcpmag.com). Nelson Ruest is a regular speaker at Comdex and other conferences in Canada and the U.S.

About Resolutions Enterprises

Resolutions Enterprises is a small Canadian consulting company focused on change management in IT. It provides architectural services to medium-to-large organizations, and specializes in Microsoft technologies. Visit us at www.Reso-Net.com.

CONTENTS

PREFACE

Twenty years ago, when most computers were mainframes or minicomputers, operators and administrators had scheduled, specific tasks they needed to perform on an ongoing basis. Each time a task was performed, they had to make note of the time and write their initials in a logbook to demonstrate when the task was performed and by whom.

Today, networks are made from loosely coupled collections of servers and workstations that may or may not include mainframes or minicomputers. Network or systems administration has become much more complex and covers many more tasks than in the past but, somehow, we've lost something in the transition. Most administrators don't keep logbooks any more. Most don't have fixed schedules for administrative activities. Many don't perform even the most basic administrative tasks.

The goal of this book is to help system administrators keep their Windows Server 2003 networks up and running, in the best of health. It outlines over 160 administrative tasks and gives the recommended frequency for each task. It is powered by a companion web site (www.Reso-Net.com/PocketAdmin), the aim of which is provide further information about and additional tools for Windows Server administration. Comments can be sent to a special e-mail address: PocketAdmin@Reso-Net.com. Enjoy!

ACKNOWLEDGMENTS

We would like to thank everyone who contributed to this book, especially Marie-Andrée Furlong for researching every task. Your contribution was invaluable.

We would also like to thank Rod Trent whose insightful comments helped make the book richer and more complete.

Thanks also go to the system administrators of Canadian National Railways in Montreal, Canada, for taking the time to review and discuss with us the final task list we collated. Your perceptiveness was extremely useful and made the book more realistic.

Thanks to VMware Corporation for providing us with the tools to create our virtual lab environment and test out every single procedure outlined here.

Thanks, in advance, to those readers who will take the time to send us their comments and their questions. You will help us make this a better book by feeding the companion web site.

INTRODUCTION

This Pocket Administrator's guide strives to be different from other guidebooks by going straight to the heart of the matter. We assume that when you reach for this book, it will not be for a long-winded explanation of how something works but because you are in the middle of a task and need answers, fast. Each task outlined here is focused on the task itself and does not usually include extensive background information.

If possible, each task description covers at least three areas:

- The graphical interface
- The command line, if available
- A recommended script, if applicable

The first area explains how you would approach the task to perform it on one or two servers. In fact, the graphical approach is designed primarily for administrators of small networks that contain less than 25 servers. The second area details how you would approach a task when you have to perform it on a series of servers. Unfortunately, even though Windows Server 2003 includes over 60 new command-line tools, this type of tool is not always available for every task. The advantage of this approach is that it is easy to insert command lines into command files in either CMD or BAT format to run them automatically. Another advantage of the command file is that it can be piped into a text file for automatic record keeping, making your task even simpler.

The third method is for extremely large networks where there are hundreds of servers. This book does not include any scripts of its own. It is linked to the Microsoft TechNet Script Center (http://www.microsoft.com/technet/treeview/default.asp?url=/technet/scriptcenter/default.asp); this center provides the building blocks for hundreds of scripts. Each time one of these scripts is applicable to a given task, it is referenced in the book through a special icon.

As you'll see, there are several tasks in this book that do not have an accompanying script on the site. This is why you should continue to check Microsoft's Web site. The Microsoft Script Center team is constantly adding new script examples. In fact, if you have an idea for a script, you can send them a request by writing to the scripting guys at HYPERLINK "mailto:scripter@microsoft.com" scripter@microsoft.com.

Using Server Roles

This book is structured in much the same way you structure your network. Chapter 1 begins with general activities—activities that must be performed on every server no matter what their role in the enterprise. In addition, this chapter covers specific one-time tasks that you need to perform to prepare your administrative environment. This should give you all the tools you need to simplify your administration.

The next chapters are loosely based on the server roles you find in the Manage Your Server interface. Seven server roles are outlined here:

- **File and Print Servers**   These servers focus on the provision of storage and structured document services to the network. These functions form the basis of Information Sharing within the network.

- **Network Infrastructure Servers**   These servers provide core networking functions such as IP addressing or name resolution including support for legacy systems. They also provide Routing and Remote Access services.

- **Identity Management Servers**   These servers are the core identity managers for the network. They contain and maintain the entire Corporate Identity Database for all Users and User Access. For Windows Server 2003, these would be servers running Active Directory Services.

- **Dedicated Web Servers** These servers focus on the provision of Web Services to user communities. This can be with Windows Server 2003, Web Edition, or with another edition running Web services.

- **Application Servers** These servers provide application services to the user community. Windows Server 2003 examples would be SQL Server, Commerce Server, and so on.

- **Terminal Servers** These servers provide a central application execution environment to users. Users need only have a minimal infrastructure to access these servers because their entire execution environment resides on the server itself.

- **Collaboration Servers** These servers provide the infrastructure for collaboration within the enterprise. Their services can include SharePoint Services, Streaming Media Services, and Real Time Communications.

TIP *These server roles are drawn from* Windows Server 2003: Best Practices for Enterprise Deployments by Ruest and Ruest, *from McGraw-Hill Osborne (2003). More information is available at www.Reso-Net.com/ WindowsServer.*

Chapter 2 covers the first server role, File and Print, because it is the most common server role. It also includes coverage of Server Clusters because these are also often put in place with file or print services in mind.

Chapter 3 covers Network Infrastructure Servers. This includes the Dynamic Host Configuration Protocol (DHCP) and the Windows Internet Naming Service (WINS). It also includes deployment servers or servers used to deploy operating systems such as Windows XP or Windows Server itself. This includes Remote Installation Services. This chapter covers two more services: Network Load Balancing as well as Remote Access and Virtual Private Networking.

Chapter 4 covers the core of the network or Identity Management. This includes two major services: Domain

Controllers and Domain Naming Servers (DNS). These two services are tied together because Active Directory relies so heavily on DNS to operate properly.

Chapter 5 covers the rest of the server roles. These include Dedicated Web Servers, Application Servers, and Terminal Servers. No Collaboration Servers are covered in this chapter since most collaboration features are add-ons to Windows Server 2003. The final portion of this chapter includes Performance and Monitoring administrative activities. Both are essential in every network.

The features covered in this book are limited by the features of Windows Server 2003 itself. Only core features available with the operating system are covered here. Though it is true that system administrators will often have to perform other administrative tasks that will vary depending on the content of their network, these tasks are beyond the scope of this book.

The Administrative Task List

The core of this book is the administrative task list. The list proposed here has been drawn from a series of different sources including our own experience as well as our clients' real-life administrative environments. It has been validated through discussion and demonstration with several system administrators. Much discussion and consultation produced the list you'll find in this book.

In addition, the task list has been categorized according to recommended task frequency. Frequencies range from a daily, weekly, and monthly, to an ad hoc basis. The latter is a category that includes everything from bi-yearly, yearly, and pretty much any time because while some tasks must be performed, their timing cannot be predicted.

TIP *If you do find that the schedule or the task list doesn't fit your needs, send us a note. Let us know what suits you best and we'll publish updated information on the Web site. Write to us at PocketAdmin@Reso-Net.com.*

The System Administrator

As a system administrator, you'll use a variety of tools to perform the activities listed here. Some of the activities will be administrative, some technical. Some will always be manual while others will be automated. Some will use Windows Server 2003's graphical interface and others, the command line.

To perform this job, you'll have to be technician, administrator, manager, communicator, operator, user, negotiator, and sometimes, director. You'll also need a significant understanding of the environment you work in and of the technologies that support it. This is why it is so important for you to gain a sound understanding in Windows Server 2003. *You are expected to be already familiar with core Windows Server features before using this book.*

System Prerequisites

The prerequisites for the task descriptions in this book are few. You should, however, have standard server builds. In fact, your servers should be designed in two steps. The first should be a general server build. This general build should include every element that is common to all servers no matter what their role. You should also take care to personalize servers and standardize their personalization. Personalization should include elements such as modified folder views to include hidden objects and a status bar, as well as adding commonly-used tools to the Quick Launch Area. Once you're finished personalizing the server, you should update the Default Profile to make sure the view is the same for each administrator that logs onto a server.

Chapter 1 lists how to perform this personalization and how to update the Default User. Make sure you perform this step and capture this personalization in your standard server build.

TIP   *Task GS-17 in Chapter 1 tells you how to build a comprehensive Microsoft Management Console for system administration. To help save you time, a copy of this console is available from the companion web site at www.Reso-Net.com/PocketAdmin.*

The second step in your server preparation process should focus on the role the server will play. Once again, you should make sure that each server playing a specific role in your network is built in the same manner at all times. This can only facilitate your work.

Organizing Your Task Schedule

The task frequency should help you organize and define an administrative schedule. You can use the Task Management feature in Microsoft Outlook to help manage your administration schedule, especially for weekly, monthly, and bi-annual tasks. You should include daily tasks in the schedule at first so that you can become familiar with them. It is a good idea to review all the tasks that are listed as "ad hoc" tasks and determine when you want to perform them.

One objective of this book is to help save you time. You might consider doing all daily tasks in the morning, then spending the afternoons of the first days of the week to perform weekly tasks. Reserve one afternoon of each week for monthly tasks; this way, you can spread them out over the course of the month. This should normally leave two afternoons per week for other, or ad hoc, tasks. Start out with this type of schedule and refine it as you go.

TIP   *The Appendix includes a list of all tasks sorted by frequency. It should help you define your administrative schedule.*

This book is a pocket book for a reason. It is designed to be used as an everyday backup tool. Use it. Carry it around with you. Make notes in the margins. Fill it with page markers and post-it notes. That's what it's designed for.

Chapter 1

General Server Administration

Though most servers will play a particular role within your organization, it is clear that some administrative tasks need to be performed on all servers no matter what their role is. These are the general server administration tasks. They include everything from making sure the server is up and running to verifying that it continues to be configured according to organizational standards. Many of the tasks are technical and several can be automated, but some are also purely administrative and do not require technology to be completed.

Administrative Activities

The general administration of Windows servers is divided into four administrative categories. These include general server, hardware, backup and restore, and remote administration. Table 1-1 outlines the administrative activities that you must perform on an ongoing basis to ensure proper operation of the services you deliver to your user community. It also identifies the frequency of each task.

You may or may not agree with the frequency of the activities outlined in Table 1-1. You may not even need to perform all of these activities because you don't use some of the services mentioned here. This is why you should personalize this book. Use a highlight marker to mark the procedure number for each of the procedures you actually will use. That way, it will be simpler and faster for you to locate the procedures you use the most.

You may also use different schedules than those listed in Table 1-1. The frequency of a task depends on a lot of characteristics such as system reliability, daily system

Procedure Number	Activity	Frequency
General Server		
GS-01	Run As Shortcuts	Daily
GS-02	General Service Status Verification	Daily
GS-03	System Event Log Verification	Daily
GS-04	Security Event Log Verification	Daily
GS-05	Service and Admin Account Management	Daily
GS-06	Activity Log Maintenance	Daily
GS-07	Uptime Report Management	Weekly
GS-08	Script Management	Weekly
GS-09	Script Certification Management	Weekly
GS-10	Antivirus Definition Update	Weekly
GS-11	Server Reboot	Weekly
GS-12	Security Policy Review/Update	Monthly
GS-13	Security Patch Verification	Monthly
GS-14	Service Pack/Hot Fix Update	Monthly
GS-15	New Software Evaluation	Monthly
GS-16	Inventory Management	Monthly
GS-17	Global MMC Creation	Ad hoc
GS-18	Automatic Antivirus Signature Reception	Ad hoc
GS-19	Scheduled Task Generation/Verification	Ad hoc
GS-20	Security Template Creation/Modification	Ad hoc
GS-21	Reference Help File Management	Ad hoc
GS-22	Server Staging	Ad hoc
GS-23	Administrative Add-on Tool Setup	Ad hoc
GS-24	Default User Profile Update	Ad hoc
GS-25	Technical Environment Review	Ad hoc
GS-26	System and Network Documentation	Ad hoc
GS-27	Service Level Agreement Management	Ad hoc

Table 1-1. General Server Administration Task List

Procedure Number	Activity	Frequency
GS-28	Troubleshooting Priority Management	Ad hoc
GS-29	Workload Review	Ad hoc
Hardware		
HW-01	Network Hardware Checkup	Weekly
HW-02	Server BIOS Management	Monthly
HW-03	Firmware and Server Management Software Update Management	Monthly
HW-04	Device Management	Ad hoc
Backup and Restore		
BR-01	System State Backup Generation	Daily
BR-02	Backup Verification	Daily
BR-03	Off-site Storage Tape Management	Weekly
BR-04	Disaster Recovery Strategy Testing	Monthly
BR-05	Restore Procedure Testing	Monthly
BR-06	Backup Strategy Review	Monthly
BR-07	Server Rebuild	Ad hoc
Remote Administration		
RA-01	Server RDC Management	Monthly
RA-02	PC RDC Management	Monthly
RA-03	User Support Through Remote Assistance	Ad hoc
RA-04	Remote Desktop Connection Shortcut and Web Access	Ad hoc

Table 1-1.   General Server Administration Task List (continued)

throughput, disk size, disk speed, processor power and so on. If the schedule outlined here doesn't fit with yours, change it.

TIP   *If you do find that the schedule doesn't fit your needs, send us a note. Let us know what suits you best and we'll publish updated frequency sheets on the companion web site (www.Reso-Net.com/PocketAdmin/). Write to us at PocketAdmin@Reso-Net.com.*

General Server Administration

By their very nature, servers are designed to support multitudes of users in the performance of their daily work. It doesn't matter if the number of users in the organization is 4 or 4,000, a system administrator's job will always be to make sure that the systems work, that they are secure and that they offer sufficient capabilities to continue providing a productive operation now and in the future.

Several of the activities required to accomplish this goal apply to all servers. Many are related to the simple continued operation of the machine itself or the way you interact with them.

GS-01: Run As Shortcuts

Activity Frequency: Daily

Working with servers often requires you to have administrative access rights to them. The access granted to Windows Server 2003 administrators is powerful indeed because it allows for complete control of a machine at the local level, a domain at the domain level, or a forest at the enterprise level. These rights must be used with care and consideration, especially because anything executing within an administrative context will automatically have all rights on a machine.

SECURITY SCAN *Because of the risk they pose to your enterprise, administrative accounts should both be renamed from the default and should have strong complex passwords, usually of more than 15 characters. Ultimately, they should be linked to smart cards for additional security.*

A virus or a worm, for example, executing within an administrative context can cause a lot more damage than within a user context. This is the reason why Run As shortcuts are so important. Because they support the execution of a command or application within a different security context, they let you use administrative access more sparingly, working normally with a user-level account, but performing administrative activities with just the right amount of access and no more—and protecting corporate assets all the while.

TIP *Any tool can be accessed through Run As. In Windows Server 2003, just right-click on the tool and select **Run As**; give the appropriate credentials and click **OK** to launch the tool. If the Run As command does not appear in the context menu, hold down the* SHIFT *key as you right-click.*

This activity is identified as a daily activity because if you design them properly, you will be using these shortcuts on a daily basis as you perform administrative activities on every server in your organization. Create as many shortcuts as you need. The advantage of Run As Shortcuts is that you choose the administrative account for it to execute under each time you launch the tool. This way you can grant each shortcut only the access it needs. And because they don't automatically run in a new context (you can't embed the account and password), they don't present a security risk in and of themselves.

SECURITY SCAN   *Using shortcuts in graphical mode is the safest way to use the Run As command.*

The following tools are useful to have as Run As Shortcuts:

- The Global Microsoft Management Console you will be creating in **Procedure GS-17**

- Windows Explorer

- The Command prompt

- The Backup Console

- Specialized tools such as the Active Directory consoles or the Group Policy Management Console

Shortcuts are more easily created on the desktop. Once created, they can be moved to the Quick Launch Area toolbar for easier access. Then you can delete them from the desktop. To create a Run As shortcut:

1. Move to the desktop. The quickest way is to click the **Desktop** icon in the **Quick Launch Area**.

2. Right-click anywhere on the desktop and select **New | Shortcut**.

3. Either click the **Browse** button to locate the command or console you want to run or type the command directly. The advantage of typing in the command is that it lets you use environment variables to locate the command or console. For example, you can use %SystemRoot% for Explorer, the Command Prompt, or the Backup Console. Click **Next** when done.

4. Click **Finish** to create the shortcut.

TIP *Alternatively, it may be easier to simply make copies of shortcuts that can be found in the All Programs menu.*

5. Once the shortcut is created, right-click on it to select **Properties**.

6. On the **General** tab, click the **Advanced** button.

7. In the Advanced dialog box, select **Run with different credentials**. Click **OK** to close the dialog box.

8. Click **OK** to close the Properties dialog box.

The shortcut is ready. Now you can move it to the Quick Launch Area. When you use the shortcut, it automatically displays the Run As dialog box. You can then choose to run it with your current credentials or select **The following user** and enter administrative credentials (see Figure 1-1).

Alternatively, you can create Run As shortcuts through the command line. Simply put it in a text file with the .cmd extension and point the shortcut to this file. The command line gives you the opportunity to refine the use of the Run As command through switches that alter its default behavior. In addition, the command line lets you create a single .cmd file that includes start commands for all of the tools you use to perform regular administrative

Figure 1-1. Using Run As to launch a program

tasks. This command file can in turn be made into a shortcut that you can locate in the Quick Launch Area.

Another advantage to this approach is the /savecred switch. This switch serves two functions: the first is to store credentials for a command, and the second is to use stored credentials. Therefore, if you use the following command structure in a command file, you can automatically start all the tools you need with the appropriate credentials assigned to each:

```
runas /user:username@domainname /savecred commandname
```

where *username@domainname* is the user principal name for the administrative account you want to use and *commandname* is the path and name of the command you want to start. The commands used to start the tools mentioned earlier should be:

```
runas /user:username@domainname /savecred "mmc
C:\Toolkit\globalmmc.msc"
runas /user:username@domainname /savecred
%SystemRoot%\explore.exe
runas /user:username@domainname /savecred
%SystemRoot%\system32\cmd.exe
runas /user:username@domainname /savecred
%SystemRoot%\system32\ntbackup.exe
```

You can use the same command structure for the other tools you deem necessary to your job and that require administrative credentials. Store the command file in the C:\Toolkit folder to make it available to all of the administrative credentials that you will be using. This folder is required because, by default, the My Documents folder is set to allow interaction from your own account and requires security modifications to allow other credentials to access its contents. More on this folder is discussed in **Procedure GS-17**.

 *Make sure you use **Procedure FS-13** to assign appropriate security parameters to the C:\Toolkit folder, especially if you create a command file that includes `runas` commands with stored credentials. Allowing anyone access to this folder is a high security risk. You should consider restricting access to the C:\Toolkit folder to only administrative level accounts and then create a Run As Shortcut to your Toolkit Command File. This way, no one will be able to inadvertently run this file through improper access to your workstation.*

Two more command switches are useful in the `runas` command. The `/smartcard` switch supports the use of smart cards for authentication. This should be used by security-conscious organizations. Smart cards are so easy to use in Windows Server 2003 that it is highly recommended that you assign them to administrative accounts. The `/netonly` switch limits the access rights to the network only and does not allow the new security context to interact with the local machine. Use both settings appropriately when working with Run As Shortcuts.

GS-02: General Service Status Verification

Activity Frequency: Daily

The very purpose of a server is to deliver services. It is deemed as functioning properly when all the services it is supposed to be delivering are up and running and in a fully functional state. This is why it is so important for you to properly document not only the specific role of each server in your network infrastructure, but also the actual services it has installed and the general state of each of these services.

TIP *A detailed Server Data Sheet can be found at the companion web site: www.Reso-Net.com/PocketAdmin. Use this sheet as the basis of your server documentation and identify installed services.*

To verify the status of services on the servers you work with:

1. Launch the **Computer Management** console (**Quick Launch Area | Computer Management**).

2. Connect to the appropriate server (**Action | Connect to another computer**) and either type in the server name (\\servername) or use the **Browse** button to locate it. Click **OK** when done.

3. Move to the **Services** window (**Services and Applications | Services**).

4. Sort the services according to status by clicking **Status** in the top of the Services window.

5. Verify against your records that all services are in the appropriate running and startup state. If some services use credentials other than Local System account, use **Procedure GS-05** to make sure these credentials are entered properly. Record and investigate any service that is not in its intended state. Verify all servers.

Alternatively, you can use the Remote Server Information command located in the Resource Kit, run it against each server you need to manage, and pipe the results into a text file:

```
srvinfo \\computername >filename.txt
```

where *computername* references the name of the server you want to investigate. If left blank, it lists information about the local server. Use *filename.txt* to identify the name and path of the file you want to send the information into. Once again, you can put a series of these commands in a command file and use **Procedure GS-19** to automatically generate the output files every day. This helps you quickly identify the state of all services in your network.

Finally, all services can be controlled through the `sc` or the `net` commands. For the latter, type `net` at the command prompt to view the list of supported commands. Type `net help` *commandname* at the command prompt to get detailed information on each command. The only drawback of this command is that it cannot be run remotely. You have to open either local or remote sessions on the server you need to manage to use these commands.

The `sc` command, on the other hand, can run on any server you have access to. Its command structure is as follows:

```
sc \\servername command servicename
```

where `\\`*servername* is the name of the server you want to access, *command* is the name of the `sc` command you want, and *servicename* is the service you want to affect. Type `sc /?` for more information.

> **SCRIPT CENTER**   *The Microsoft TechNet Script Center includes a series of Windows Scripting Host (WSH) sample scripts that help you perform service administration tasks. These scripts can be found at http://www.microsoft.com/technet/treeview/ default.asp?url=/technet/scriptcenter/services/ default.asp?frame=true*

GS-03: System Event Log Verification

✔ **Activity Frequency:**   **Daily**

Another useful diagnostic tool is the System Event Log. It details information about general server health and operation. Each significant event is recorded and an event description is entered. Events can be in one of three states:

Information: An event has occurred and it is significant enough to be recorded. These events usually record normal operation of the server.

 Warning: A noncritical error has occurred and warrants a record in the Event Log. Watch these event types carefully because they can quickly become errors.

 Error: A critical error has occurred and should be investigated and repaired. All of these events must lead to investigation and repair. Windows Server 2003 will often list detailed information about avenues of investigation.

To verify the System Event Log on the servers you work with:

1. Launch the **Computer Management** console (**Quick Launch Area | Computer Management**).

2. Connect to the appropriate server (**Action | Connect to another computer**) and either type in the server name (\\servername) or use the **Browse** button to locate it. Click **OK** when done.

3. Move to the **System Event Log** (**System Tools | Event Viewer | System**).

4. Identify any errors or warnings. Take appropriate action if either appears.

Make note of any corrective action you need to take. Use **Procedure GS-06** to log the different events you investigate each day.

You can also reset the size of each Event Log. To do so, right-click on the log name in the left pane of the MMC and select **Properties**. Set **Maximum Log Size** and **Maximum Log Size Events** appropriately for your needs.

SCRIPT CENTER   *The Microsoft TechNet Script Center includes a series of WSH sample scripts that help you perform Event Log administration tasks. These scripts can be found at http://www.microsoft.com/ technet/treeview/default.asp?url=/technet/scriptcenter/ logs/default.asp?frame=true.*

GS-04: Security Event Log Verification

Activity Frequency: Daily

If your organization has decided to enable access auditing, it will be important for you to verify the Security Event Log on a daily basis to ensure that there are no untoward events occurring in your network.

Auditing is enabled through Group Policy. The Audit Policy is located in the security settings of Group Policy. Enabling the Audit Policy can have significant impact in your network. Audited objects and events slow down the system, so it is important to audit only those events or objects you deem critical in your network.

SECURITY SCAN *By default, all audit events are turned on in Windows Server 2003; therefore, you only need to further refine and add to the objects you want to verify. In addition, the Security Event Log is defined at 132MB and overwrites as needed once the log is full.*

To define or review the Audit Policy:

1. Use **Procedure DC-16** to edit the appropriate Group Policy Object (GPO). This is usually a GPO that applies to all objects in the domain.

2. In the Group Policy Editor, select **Computer Configuration | Windows Settings | Security Settings | Audit Policy**.

3. Double-click on the event you want to audit and modify the policy. You can audit either the success or the failure of an event or both.

4. Document each setting you change.

TIP *A Group Policy Documentation Spreadsheet is available on the companion web site at www.Reso-Net.com/ PocketAdmin.*

To audit object access, such as a container in AD or a file
on a server, you must then turn on auditing for that object
and identify who you want to audit. To do so:

1. Locate the object you want to audit. Try to audit
   containers such as folders or organizational units
   rather than individual objects.

2. Right-click on it to select **Properties**. Move to the
   Security tab.

3. Click the **Advanced** button. In AD, you must enable
   Advanced Features from the **View** menu of the AD
   consoles to do this.

4. Identify which groups you want to audit. It is usually
   easier to select all-encompassing groups such as
   Authenticated Users than to use more specific groups.
   It all depends on who and what you are auditing.

5. From now on, access events will be monitored in the
   Security Event Log.

Document all the changes you make. To view audit results:

1. Launch the **Computer Management** console (**Quick
   Launch Area | Computer Management**).

2. Connect to the appropriate server (**Action |
   Connect to another computer**) and either type in
   the server name (\\servername) or use the **Browse**
   button to locate it. Click **OK** when done.

3. Move to the **Security Event Log** (**System Tools |
   Event Viewer | Security**).

4. Identify any success or failures. Take appropriate
   action if you identify inappropriate actions.

Make note of any corrective action you need to take. Use
Procedure GS-06 to log the different events you investigate
each day.

You can also reset the size of the Security Event Log.
Follow the last part of **Procedure GS-03** to do so.

TIP *If you set the log file to lock (**Do not overwrite events**) once it reaches maximum log size and you fear it hasn't been backed up, you will automatically shut down the server until the log file is cleared.*

GS-05: Service and Admin Account Management

> ✔ **Activity Frequency:** **Daily**

Administrative accounts are high-priced commodities in every network. Gone are the days when they had to be handed out generally to almost anyone who complained loud enough. In today's Windows Server 2003 network, you can and should define just the right amount of access rights for each and everyone who interacts with your system. Therefore, you should have very few administrative accounts at the domain or forest level and have many more specialty administrative accounts that focus on granting just the right amount of access to do a specific job. These accounts and the accesses they grant should be managed or at least reviewed on a daily basis.

Several procedures support the assignation of appropriate rights and permissions to administrative accounts. Some are assigned through the integration of built-in security groups such as Server or Backup Operators, while others are assigned through the association with User Rights Assignment policies to the accounts, or rather the groups that contain these accounts. Three tools support the assignation of appropriate rights:

- Active Directory Users and Computers to create the accounts and assign them to either built-in or custom administrative groups

- Group Policy Management Console to locate and edit the appropriate GPO

- Group Policy Editor to actually assign the user rights

In addition, you might use the Computer Management console to assign local rights to domain groups and accounts.

To modify user rights, use **Procedure DC-16** to edit the appropriate GPO, usually one that will affect all of the objects you want to modify. Locate the **User Rights Assignment** setting (**Computer Policy I Security Settings I Local Policies I User Rights Assignment**) and assign appropriate settings to administrative accounts. Remember, it is always easier to assign rights to a group than to individual objects, thus it is a good idea to regroup administrative accounts into administrative groups. Use **Procedure DC-16** again to ensure proper use of these accounts.

In addition, in today's enterprise network, you must also manage service accounts—accounts that are granted enough administrative privilege to support the operation of specific services in your network. For example, you might use service accounts to run antivirus engines or scheduled tasks (see **Procedure GS-19**). The advantage of using a service account to operate a given service or automated task is that you can also use the Security Event Log to review the proper operation of the service. A success event is written in this log each time the service uses its privileged access or logs on.

Service accounts in particular must have specific settings and properties:

- Account must have a complex name

- Account must have a complex password at least 15 characters long

- Password never expires

- User cannot change password

- Act as part of the operating system right

- Log on as a service

 **SECURITY SCAN** *The last two settings should be applied with alacrity, especially* **Act as part of the operating system**, *because they grant extremely high access levels to the service.*

The last two settings must be set in a GPO under the **User Rights Assignment** settings. Remember to regroup service accounts into service groups as well.

Service accounts present the additional operational overhead of requiring regular password changes. This cannot be limited to simply changing the password in Active Directory Users and Computers because when service accounts are assigned to services, you must give them the account's password for the service to work properly. This means you also need to modify the password in the service Properties dialog box. Use **Procedure GS-02** to do so.

> *SCRIPT CENTER* *The Microsoft TechNet Script Center includes a WSH sample script that lets you change service account passwords. This script can be found at http://www.microsoft.com/technet/treeview/ default.asp?url=/technet/scriptcenter/services/ scrsvc01.asp?frame=true. It also lets you change administrative user account passwords. A series of scripts affecting user accounts can be found at http:// www.microsoft.com/technet/treeview/default.asp?url=/ technet/scriptcenter/user/default.asp?frame=true.*

GS-06: Activity Log Maintenance

Activity Frequency: **Daily**

Part of your job is also to record both what you do and what you need to do to maintain or repair the network on an ongoing basis. This is the reason why you should keep a Daily Activity Log. Ideally, this log will be electronic and transportable so that you can make annotations whenever you need to. It can be stored in either a Tablet PC or a Pocket PC that you carry with you at all times. The Tablet PC is more useful because it supports a fully working version of Windows and allows you to run both Windows Server 2003 help files (see **Procedure GS-21**) or run virtual machines to simulate problematic situations. In addition, Microsoft OneNote is ideally suited to logging daily activities.

If both devices are unattainable, you should at least use a paper logbook that you carry at all times. You can maintain this log as best suits you, but it is sometimes better to note activities as you perform them than to wait for a specific time of day.

TIP *A sample Daily Activity Log can be found on the companion web site at www.Reso-net.com/PocketAdmin.*

GS-07: Uptime Report Management

Once a week, you'll need to produce an uptime report for all servers. This helps you track the status of various servers and identify which configurations are best in your environment. There are several tools you can use to produce these reports.

The last line in the report generated by the `srvinfo` command used in **Procedure GS-02** identifies how long a server has been in operation. A second command, `systeminfo`, gives you information on the server you are examining as well as how long it has been running. A third tool, `uptime`, is designed specifically to report on server uptime. This tool is available as a download only. Search for `uptime` at www.microsoft.com/download.

Using the last tool and a little ingenuity, you can produce your uptime reports automatically:

1. Download and install **uptime.exe** into the C:\Toolkit folder.

2. Create a command file that contains the following code line, one for each server in your network:

   ```
   uptime \\servername
   ```

3. Save the command file when done.

4. Use **Procedure GS-19** to assign the command file to a weekly schedule task.

5. In the scheduled task, use the following command to assign output to a text file:

   ```
   commandfile.cmd >filename.txt
   ```

The `uptime` command will thus create the report for you every week. All you have to do is locate the output file and review the results.

SCRIPT CENTER   *The Microsoft TechNet Script Center includes two scripts related to system uptime management. The first is Determining System Uptime and the second is Monitoring System Uptime. Both can be found at http://www.microsoft.com/technet/ treeview/ default.asp?url=/technet/scriptcenter/monitor/ default.asp?frame=true.*

GS-08: Script Management

Activity Frequency: Weekly

Scripts running in the Windows Script Host are an essential part of Windows network administration. As you know and begin to realize, scripting in Windows is a world of its own. The scripting language has evolved to the point where a script is a sophisticated program that can be run in either graphic (intended for users) or character mode (administrative scripts). Running a script in either mode is controlled by the command you use to activate it:

```
wscript scriptname
cscript scriptname
```

where `wscript` runs it in graphical mode and `cscript` runs it in character mode.

With the coming of script viruses such as ILOVEYOU.vbs, you should make sure the scripts you run are secure. The best way to do so is to sign your scripts with a digital certificate. First you'll need to obtain the certificate. This can be done from a third-party certificate authority, or it can be done by yourself if you decide to use your own certificate server (a server function available in Windows Server 2003). Use **Procedure DC-11** to do so.

1

SCRIPT CENTER *Signing a script with a certificate is a programmatic activity. Sample signature addition and management scripts are available at the Microsoft TechNet Script Center at http:// www.microsoft.com/ technet/treeview/default.asp?url=/ technet/scriptcenter/monitor/default.asp?frame=true.*

SECURITY SCAN *You can also encode scripts to protect them. You can find the Microsoft Script Encoder at http://msdn.microsoft.com/ scripting/vbscript/download/x86/sce10en.exe.*

Every script you create and sign should be fully documented. This documentation should include all pertinent information on the script and should be reviewed and kept up-to-date on a weekly basis.

TIP *A sample Script Management Log can be found on the companion web site.*

SCRIPT CENTER *You can use a script to document the contents of another script. Sample code is available at the Microsoft TechNet Script Center at http:// www.microsoft.com/technet/treeview/ default.asp?url=/technet/scriptcenter/other/ ScrOth03.asp?frame=true.*

Writing scripts can be challenging when you aren't familiar with either the Windows Management Instrumentation (WMI) or the Active Directory Services Interface (ADSI). This is why it is a great idea to use the Microsoft Scriptomatic utility to generate scripts for you. Scriptomatic is available from the Microsoft Download Center. Just search for Scriptomatic at www.microsoft.com/ downloads. In addition, a good scripting primer is available at http://msdn.microsoft.com/library/en-us/dnclinic/ html/scripting06112002.asp.

Installing Scriptomatic is simply a matter of unzipping the file from the downloaded compressed archive. You should store the scriptomatic.hta file in the C:\ToolKit folder. You can also use a Run As shortcut (see **Procedure GS-01**) to execute Scriptomatic and place it in the Quick Launch Area.

To write a script with Scriptomatic:

1. Launch **scriptomatic.hta** or your **Run As shortcut**.

2. In Scriptomatic, select the WMI class you want to work with. Each class is named Win32_. You only need to pay attention to the last part of the class name. For example, to write a script that lets you view the status of every service, select the Win32_Service class. Scriptomatic automatically generates the proper script (see Figure 1-2).

3. Click **Run**. Scriptomatic will launch a command console to run the script.

4. Click **Save** to save the script to a file (VBS extention).

You can use these scripts to perform administrative tasks and capture the output. To do so, use the following command:

```
cscript scriptname.vbs >filename.txt
```

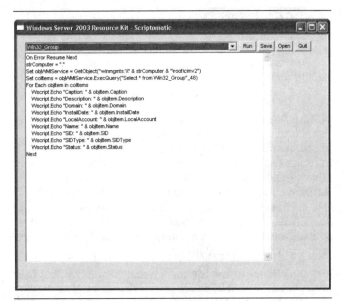

Figure 1-2. To generate a script listing local groups on a computer, select the Win32 Group class in Scriptomatic.

where *scriptname.vbs* is the name of the script you want
to run and *filename.txt* is the name of the output file you
want to create. You can use **Procedure GS-19** to place this
command in a scheduled task and run it on a regular basis.

You can use Scriptomatic to help you generate your logon
script. You may need to combine portions of a WMI script
with portions of an ADSI script to generate a complete
logon script. Use **Procedure DC-31** to do so.

In addition to a logon script, you may also want to display
a pre-logon message to your users. This helps make sure
users are forewarned of the legal consequences of the
misuse of IT equipment and information. Once again, this
is done through a GPO. Use **Procedure DC-16** to edit the
appropriate GPO and modify the following settings to
display a logon message:

- **User Configuration | Windows Settings | Security
  Settings | Local Policies | Security Options |
  Interactive Logon**: Message title for users attempting
  to log on

- **User Configuration | Windows Settings | Security
  Settings | Local Policies | Security Options |
  Interactive Logon**: Message text for users attempting
  to log on

GS-09: Script Certification Management

Activity Frequency: **Weekly**

The best way to make sure only signed scripts can run in
your network is to use Software Restriction Policies (SRP).
SRP provide script and program verification in one of four
ways:

- Hash rules
- Certificate rules
- Path rules
- Internet zone rules

The two safest and simplest to use are hash and/or
certificate rules. Both can be applied to scripts and
programs such as corporate installation packages (usually
in the Windows Installer or .msi format). Here's how to
apply or verify certificate-based SRP rules:

1. Use **Procedure DC-16** to edit the appropriate GPO.
   It should apply to all targeted systems.

2. Right-click on **Software Restriction Policies**
   (**Computer Configuration** | **Windows Settings** |
   Security Settings | **Software Restriction Policies**)
   and select **New Software Restriction Policies** from
   the context menu. This generates the SRP
   environment.

3. Make sure that **Software Restriction Policies** are
   expanded in the left pane, then right-click on
   Additional Rules and select **New Certificate Rule**.

4. In the New Certificate Rule dialog box, click **Browse**
   to locate the certificate you use to sign both installation
   packages and scripts, select **Unrestricted** as the
   security level, and type a description. Click **OK**
   when done.

5. Move to **Software Restriction Policies** and select
   Designated File Types from the right pane. You will
   note that both .wsh and .msi are already listed as
   restricted extensions. Click **OK** to close the dialog box.

6. Select **Trusted Publishers** in the same location.
   Make sure **End users** are able to accept certificates
   and that both **Publisher** and **Timestamp** are
   checked. Click **OK** when done.

7. Select **Enforcement** to review that .dll files are not
   verified and that this setting applies to **All users**.

 **SECURITY SCAN** *You may decide to remove local
administrators from being
affected by this rule, but do so very carefully.*

8. Document all your changes.

GS-10: Antivirus Definition Update

Activity Frequency: **Weekly**

SECURITY SCAN   *Virus protection is a key element of an integrated defense system. Thus, it is essential to make sure it is working properly on an ongoing basis.*

This is the first placeholder task. It is here because you need to perform this task on servers no matter what, but it isn't a core Windows Server 2003 task.

Three tasks are required on a weekly basis for virus protection management:

- Check virus management logs to make sure no viruses have been found in the last day.

- Check your Virus Management console to determine that your virus signatures are up-to-date. Reconfigure the update schedule if it is not appropriate or if threats increase.

- Perform random virus scans on file shares, applications, and system drives to make sure they are not infected.

Use the Virus Management console to set the appropriate settings. In some virus engines, most of these tasks can be automated and consoles can alert you if new viruses are found.

TIP   *Make sure the antivirus engine you use is compatible with Windows Server 2003. In fact, it would ideally be certified for this platform.*

GS-11: Server Reboot

Activity Frequency: **Weekly**

Since the delivery of Windows NT by Microsoft, especially NT version 4 in 1996, most systems administrators have found it wise to regularly reboot servers running this operating system to clear out random access memory and to generally refresh the system. Since then, Microsoft has invested significant effort to limit and even completely avoid this procedure.

TIP *It is strongly recommended that you begin by examining how Windows Server 2003 operates within your network before you continue to use this practice. You will find that WS03 servers no longer require regular reboots. In fact, you will be surprised at the level of service you can achieve with this operating system. This will be in evidence in the uptime reports you produce in* **Procedure GS-07***.*

If you do feel you need to perform this activity on a regular basis, you can use the shutdown command from the command line to remotely shut down and reboot servers. The following command shuts down and reboots a remote server:

```
shutdown -r -f -m \\servername
```

where -r requests a reboot, -f forces running applications to close and -m specifies the machine you want to shut down. As with all character mode commands, you can create a command file that includes a command for each server you want to shut down. If you put the shutdown commands in a command file, you should also use the -c switch to add a message to the command:

```
shutdown -r -f -m \\servername -c "Weekly Reboot Time"
```

Use **Procedure GS-19** to assign the command file to a schedule task.

TIP *The shutdown command automatically bypasses the Shutdown Event Tracker—a dialog box you must normally complete when shutting down a server running Windows Server 2003. Therefore, be sure to keep a shutdown log to document your automated shutdowns.*

The Shutdown Event Tracker is a tool Windows Server 2003 uses to log shutdown and reboot information. It stores its information in the %SystemRoot%\System32\ LogFiles\Shutdown folder. It can be controlled through two GPO settings:

- **Computer Configuration I Administrative Templates I System I Display Shutdown Event Tracker**

- **Computer Configuration I Administrative Templates I System I Activate Shutdown Event Tracker System State Data feature**

Use **Procedure DC-16** to modify the appropriate GPO. This GPO should affect all servers.

SCRIPT CENTER   *The Microsoft Technet Script Center includes a sample script for restarting a computer at http://www.microsoft.com/technet/treeview/ default.asp?url=/technet/scriptcenter/compmgmt/ ScrCM38.asp?frame=true.*

GS-12: Security Policy Review/Update

Activity Frequency: **Monthly**

The security policy is the one tool that is at the core of your security program. It determines everything, including how you respond to security breaches and how you protect yourself from them. It serves to identify which common security standards you wish to implement within your organization. These involve both technical and nontechnical policies and procedures. An example of a technical policy would be the security parameters you will set at the staging of each computer in your organization. A nontechnical policy would deal with the habits users should develop to select complex passwords and protect them. Finally, you will need to identify the parameters for each policy you define.

TIP   *A sample list of the items found in a security policy can be found on the companion web site at www.Reso-Net.com/PocketAdmin.*

Your monthly verification of the security policy should include a review of all of its items and answer questions such as:

- How effective is your user communications program? Should you enhance it?

- How effective are your security strategies? Should they be reinforced?

- Is your administrative staff following all security principles?

- Are there potential breaches that have not been identified?

- Is new technology secure? What is its impact on your global security strategy?

Document and communicate all changes you make during this review.

GS-13: Security Patch Verification

Activity Frequency: Monthly

Security patches are a fact of life in any enterprise computing environment. But if your operating systems are designed properly and your servers run only the services required to support their role, you can most likely limit your available security patch verification to a monthly review.

Windows and Microsoft offer several tools and techniques to perform this activity. Microsoft offers email notification for security bulletins. You can register for this and other Microsoft newsletters at register.microsoft.com/regsys/pic.asp. You will require a Microsoft Passport to do so. If you don't have one, follow the instructions on the site to get one. If you don't want to use a Passport, use the link http://register.microsoft.com/subscription/subscribeme.asp?ID=135 to sign up. There is also a hot fix and security bulletin that provides useful information. It can be found at hot fix and security bulletin search: http://www.microsoft.com/technet/security/current.asp.

Microsoft isn't the only organization to send out security bulletins. An excellent source for this type of information is the SANS Institute. You can subscribe to SANS newsletters at www.sans.org/newsletters. Another useful source on heterogeneous technologies is the CERT Coordination Center (Cert/CC), which can be found at http://www.cert.org/.

In addition, Windows Server 2003 includes automated updates. This means it can predownload hot fixes and updates and tell you when they are ready for installation. This feature can be modified to tell all machines in your network to obtain patch information from a central intranet server. Once again, these are GPO settings. They are located in **Computer Configuration I Administrative Templates I Windows Components I Windows Update** and include:

- **Configure Automatic Updates:** In a corporate environment, you should use setting 4 to download and install updates according to a fixed monthly schedule.

- **Specify intranet Microsoft update service location:** Name the server from which updates will be downloaded; use the server's full DNS name.

- **No auto-restart for scheduled Automatic Updates installations:** Use this setting to stop servers from restarting after update installation. Servers can be restarted on a more regular basis with **Procedure GS-11**.

Use **Procedure DC-16** to edit the appropriate GPO. This GPO should apply to servers only. Another GPO should be set similarly for workstations, but preferably using a different intranet source server. These settings should be used in conjunction with **Microsoft Software Update Services** (SUS). Use the SUS server to validate the security fixes and updates you require in your corporate environment. Document all your changes.

TIP *To download and install SUS, search for Microsoft Software Update Services at www.microsoft.com/download.*

You can also use the Microsoft Baseline Security Analyzer (MBSA) to analyze the hot fix and service pack status of your systems. MBSA is available at the Microsoft Download web site. Search for MBSA at www.microsoft.com/downloads.

TIP *You need MBSA version 1.1.1 or greater to scan servers running Windows Server 2003.*

Since the MBSA setup file is a Windows Installer file, you can install it interactively or you can use **Procedure DC-15** to install it to several target systems. MBSA can be used to scan a single system or to scan a complete network. It will even scan network segments based on IP address ranges.

To scan a system:

1. Launch **MBSA** (**Start Menu | All Programs | Microsoft Baseline Security Analyzer**).

2. Select **Scan a computer**.

3. Use either the computer name or its IP address and select the options you want to use in the scan. Click **Start scan**.

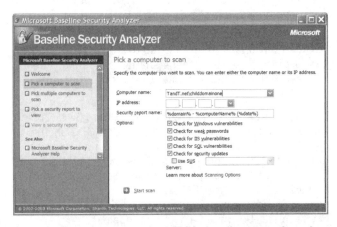

4. View the report in the MBSA details pane when the scan is complete. The report is automatically saved with the domain name, computer name and date in the \%UserProfile\Security Scans folder directly under Documents and Settings.

Store these reports very carefully because they detail sensitive information about your systems.

GS-14: Service Pack/Hot Fix Update

Activity Frequency: **Monthly**

Once an update has been approved in the SUS server, it will install automatically on all targeted systems if you have set your GPOs appropriately (see **Procedure GS-13**). The best way to run SUS is to have two environments, the production environment and a test lab. Have a few test machines (PCs and servers) linked to the test lab server.

TIP Software Update Services only verifies and updates either critical or security patches. If you want to make sure your systems also include hardware, driver and other types of updates, you will need to use the Windows Update web site at http://v4.windowsupdate.microsoft.com/ fr/default.asp.

Use the test lab to approve updates:

1. Launch the **SUS Console** on the test server by going to http://servername/SUSAdmin where *servername* is the DNS name of your SUS test server.

2. Click **Approve Updates** to review available updates. Sort the updates based on **Status**. Check the ones that apply to your environment.

3. Click the **Approve** button to apply each of the updates you checked. Wait until they are applied on your test machines, and reboot them if required.

4. Verify the proper operation of the test systems after application. If there is a problem, remove the updates one by one until the problem is corrected to identify the faulty update. Retry the remaining updates. Note the updates to approve.

5. Move to your **Production SUS Server** and approve updates for distribution to your production systems.

Hot fixes and updates install automatically through SUS, but this is not the case for service packs. These tend to require more extensive deployment preparation for installation. Their preparation involves much more thorough testing than hot fixes because service packs affect so many areas of a server. Once a service pack is assessed and approved, use **Procedure DC-15** to deploy it (unless you use a more robust deployment tool such as SMS).

> *SCRIPT CENTER* The Microsoft TechNet Script Center includes several scripts related to hot fix and service pack administration (Enumerate Installed Hot Fixes and Identify the Latest Installed Service Pack) at http://www.microsoft.com/technet/treeview/ default.asp?url=/technet/scriptcenter/compmgmt/ default.asp?frame=true.

GS-15: New Software Evaluation

Activity Frequency: Monthly

Once a month, you should also take the time to review new administration software. The objective of this task is to see if you can reduce your workload by integrating a new operational product. A good example of a highly productive operational tool is Microsoft Operations Management Server (MOM). MOM is highly effective because it monitors system events on servers and automatically corrects potentially damaging behavior as well as notifying you of the correction.

On the other hand, if your shop is of a size that does not warrant as sophisticated a tool as MOM, you might prefer to search for another tool with similar capabilities. Many of the automated administrative tasks you perform can be done through scripts, as you have already seen in a number of the tasks described previously. They can also be done with low-cost or public domain tools. Two good sources of tool information are www.MyITForum.com and www.TechRepublic.com.

Make sure you do not acquire tools that are significantly different in usage from one another. This will limit the number of tools or interfaces you and your fellow administrators will need to learn. Document any new addition to your network.

SCRIPT CENTER *Alternatively, you can use a script from the Microsoft TechNet Script Center to monitor specific events in the Event Log and generate alerts when they occur. This script can be found at http:// www.microsoft.com/technet/treeview/default.asp?url=/ technet/scriptcenter/monitor/ScrMon21.asp?frame=true.*

GS-16: Inventory Management

Activity Frequency: **Monthly**

One of the tasks you should perform on at least a monthly basis is inventory management. This includes both hardware and software inventories. You may or may not have an inventory management tool such as Systems Management Server in your network. If you do, great; your task is done. If you don't, you'll need to use other tools.

Microsoft offers the Microsoft Inventory Analysis (MSIA) tool. It does not manage the inventory for all software, but, at least, it manages all Microsoft software. To download the MSIA, search for it at www.microsoft.com/downloads.

MSIA is a wizard-based tool that lets you perform three tasks:

- Scan a local computer for Microsoft products.

- Prepare a command-line input file that includes all of the scan settings you want to use.

- Run a scan using a previously prepared command-line input file.

In addition, it lets you scan local systems, remote systems or an entire network all at once. Installation is based on the Windows Installer service. You can install it interactively or use **Procedure DC-15** to install it on target computers.

To create a command-line input file:

1. Launch **MSIA** (**Start Menu | All Programs | Microsoft Software Inventory Analyzer**). Click **Next**.

2. Select **Scan using Custom settings** and **Create Custom settings**. Click **Browse** to select the output

folder and name the output file. It will have a .cli extension for command-line input. Click **Save** to create the file. Click **Next** to continue.

3. Select the scope of the scan: Local Computer, Network or Report Consolidation. Click **Next**.

If you select Network, you will need to provide proper credentials to run the scan on all systems.

4. In the Download Database Files dialog box, click **Download**. MSIA will go to the MS Web site and download the latest data files for MS products. You will be prompted to accept a Microsoft certificate for the installation of the database. Click **Yes**. Click **OK** when the download is complete. Click **Next**.

5. Select the products you want to scan for and click **Add**. (You can use CTRL-click to select more than one product.) Check **Save these products as the default** and then click **Next**.

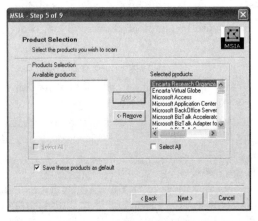

6. Select the report format(s). Click **Browse** to select the report folder and name the report file. Click **Save** to create the file. Click **Next** to continue.

7. You can choose to consolidate summary reports. These are useful for management. Click **Next**.

8. You can select to send the summary report by email to someone (or you can send it later). If you need to send it to a group, create a distribution group and enter its email address here. Do not check **Save settings as default** because you are creating a command-line input file.

9. Click **Finish** to close the command-line input file.

To run an MSIA scan:

1. Launch **MSIA** (**Start Menu | All Programs | Microsoft Software Inventory Analyzer**). Click **Next**.

2. Select **Scan using Custom settings** and **Load existing Custom settings**. If the file displayed is not the file you want to use, click **Browse** to select the folder and file you require. Click **Open** to load the file. Click **Next** to continue.

3. MSIA scans the systems based on the file settings.

4. Check **View Reports Now** and click **Finish**.

This is a great tool for verifying the inventory of Microsoft software.

SCRIPT CENTER The Microsoft TechNet Script Center includes two useful scripts for inventory management: Enumerate Installed Software at http://www.microsoft.com/technet/treeview/default.asp?url=/technet/scriptcenter/compmgmt/scrcm16.asp?frame=true and Inventory Computer Hardware at http://www.microsoft.com/technet/treeview/default.asp?url=/technet/scriptcenter/compmgmt/ScrCM30.asp?frame=true.

GS-17: Global MMC Creation

Activity Frequency: Ad hoc

Administration and management is performed through the Microsoft Management Console in Windows Server 2003. The most useful of these is the Computer Management console found in Administrative Tools. You can also right-click on the **My Computer** icon to select Manage from the context menu.

But while this is a good general-purpose console, it is not an all-encompassing tool. Thus, one of the ad hoc administrative activities you need to perform is the creation of a Global Management Console that will include all the snap-ins you require in a single MMC. In addition to all the features of the Computer Management console, this console should include the following snap-ins:

- .NET Framework 1.1 Configuration
- The three Active Directory snap-ins
- Authorization Manager
- Certification Authority (you must specify the server to manage)
- Component Services
- Distributed File System
- Group Policy Management (requires GPMC installation)
- Performance Logs and Alerts
- Remote Desktops
- Resultant Set of Policy
- Security Configuration and Analysis
- Security Templates
- Wireless Monitor

To create this console:

1. Use **Start** | **Run** to execute the following command:

   ```
   mmc /a %SystemRoot%\system32\compmgmt.msc
   ```

2. This launches the Computer Management console in editing mode. Begin by using **File** | **Save As** to save the console as **Global MMC.msc** under the C:\Toolkit folder.

3. Then use **File** | **Add/Remove Snap-in** to open the dialog box, make sure you choose **Computer**

Management under **Snap-ins added to**, and click the **Add** button.

4. Double-click each of the snap-ins listed earlier. Click **Close** when done.

5. Click **OK** to return to the console.

6. Click **File | Options**, name the console **Global MMC Console**, make sure it is set to **User mode - full access** and uncheck **Do not save changes to this console**. Click **OK** when done.

7. Use **File | Save** to save your changes.

There are several uses to this console as you will see, but it is basically the most common tool you will use to manage your network of servers.

Create a shortcut to this console using **Procedure GS-01** and store it on the Quick Launch Area toolbar.

 **SECURITY SCAN** *Secure this template thoroughly because it is powerful, indeed.*

GS-18: Automatic Antivirus Signature Reception

Activity Frequency: **Ad hoc**

This is another placeholder activity. It is essential in any antivirus strategy. It deals with the configuration of your antivirus signature update agent to recover signature updates and deliver them to all PCs and servers in your network.

This is a one-time task that cannot go unmentioned in a list of server administrative tasks.

It should be supplemented with regular spot checks on various systems to ensure the proper functioning of your antivirus signature update server.

GS-19: Scheduled Task Generation/Verification

Activity Frequency: Ad hoc

The Task Scheduler is one of the tools administrators cannot live without because it serves to automate recurring tasks in a network. Windows Server 2003's Task Scheduler is located under Control Panel in the Windows Explorer. It can also be found as the first shared element of each server's My Network Places.

Adding a share task means using the Add Scheduled Task Wizard:

1. Double-click on **Add Scheduled Task** (**Windows Explorer** | **My Computer** | **Control Panel** | **Scheduled Tasks**). Click **Next**.

2. Select the task from the list or click **Browse** to locate it on disk. Tasks can be applications, but they can also be either scripts or command files. Click **Next**.

3. Name the task and select its frequency. Click **Next**.

4. Select the **Time**, when to perform it, and a **Start date**. Click **Next**.

5. Type in the appropriate credentials and password. Click **Next**.

6. Check **Open advanced properties for this task when I click Finish** and click **Finish**.

7. In the task's Property sheet, refine the task's schedule. Use the **Schedule** tab to apply multiple schedules to the task if necessary. Use the **Settings** tab to make sure the task is configured to your corporate standards. Click **OK** when done.

You can also use the schtasks command on each server to verify the status of scheduled tasks. Use the following command:

```
schtasks /query /s computername
```

where *computername* is either the DNS name or IP address of a server. Use `schtasks /?` for more information. Once again, you can use the steps outlined at the end of **Procedure GS-07** to generate an automatic report on all servers.

SCRIPT CENTER *The Microsoft TechNet Script Center includes four different scripts for the management of scheduled tasks at http:// www.microsoft.com/ technet/treeview/default.asp?url=/ technet/scriptcenter/schedule/default.asp?frame=true.*

GS-20: Security Template Creation/Modification

Security templates are used to assign security properties to servers. Since they are assigned as Local Policies, they should contain only basic security settings such as file, registry, and service security. Create your security templates from existing templates. Microsoft provides a series of decent templates with the Windows Server 2003 Security Guide (search for it at www.microsoft.com/ download) that you can use as starters.

SECURITY SCAN *Along with GPOs, security templates and security configuration are one of the key ways you can ensure your servers remain secure.*

To create your own security templates:

1. Launch the **Global MMC Console** created in **Procedure GS-17**. Move to **Security Templates**. Templates are located in the %SystemRoot%\ security\templates directory.

2. To create a new template from an existing template, right-click on it to select **Save As** and rename it. Once it has been renamed, you can add your own settings.

3. Move to your new template and modify its settings. Begin by right-clicking on the template name and selecting **Set Description** to modify the description. Type in the appropriate information and click **OK**.

4. Expand the template to view its components and modify them as needed. Make sure you right-click on the template name and select **Save** before you exit the console.

Templates are used for a variety of purposes. They can be used to assign security settings to servers or they can be used to analyze actual settings against those stored in the template. Both can be performed in either graphical or character modes. To analyze or reset a server in graphical mode:

1. Launch the **Global MMC Console** created in **Procedure GS-17**.

2. Right-click on **Security Configuration and Analysis** and select **Open database**.

3. In the Open database dialog box, either locate the appropriate database or type in a new database name, and then click **OK**. The default path setting is **My Documents\Security\Databases**.

4. Select the appropriate template from the available list and click **OK**.

5. To analyze your system, right-click on **Security Configuration and Analysis** and select **Analyze Computer now**.

6. Since every analysis or configuration operation requires a log file, a dialog box appears to ask you the location of the log file. The default path setting is **My Documents\Security\Logs** and the default name is the same as the database. Either type in the name of a new log file, use the **Browse** button to locate an existing file, or click **OK** to accept the default name. The analysis will begin.

7. Once the analysis is complete, you can see the difference in settings between the template and

the computer. Simply move to a setting you wish to view and select it. Differences (if any) will be displayed in the right pane.

8. You can modify database settings to conform to the values you want to apply by moving to the appropriate value and double-clicking on it. Select **Define this policy in the database**, modify the setting, and click **OK**. Repeat for each setting you need to modify.

9. Use the right-mouse button to display the **Security Configuration and Analysis** context menu and select **Save** to save the modifications you make to the database.

10. To configure a computer with the settings in the database, select **Configure Computer now** from the same context menu. Once again, you will need to specify the location and name of the log file before the configuration can begin.

Alternatively, you can use the `secedit` command to perform these tasks at the command line. Use the following command to configure a system:

```
secedit /configure /db filename.sdb /log filename.log
/areas REGKEYS FILESTORE SERVICES /quiet
```

Use the following command to analyze a system:

```
secedit /analyze /db filename.sdb /log
filename.log /quiet
```

The latter can be set in a scheduled task using **Procedure GS-19**. Use `secedit /?` for more information.

GS-21: Reference Help File Management

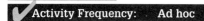

Activity Frequency: Ad hoc

Another ad hoc activity is the installation of server help files on your own system. Installing server help files locally can be very useful since it gives you easy access to a wealth of server information. This is done through the Windows XP/Server 2003 Help and Support Center (H&SC) and requires the Windows Server 2003 installation CD:

1. Launch the **Help and Support Center** on your system and click the **Options** button at the top.

2. Click **Install and Share Windows Help** in the left window pane. Click **Install Help content from a CD or disk image**.

3. Type in the drive letter for your CD reader and click **Find**.

4. Select the help you want to install and click **Install**.

5. Once installed, you can click **Switch from one operating system's Help content to another**, select the operating system you want, and click **Switch**.

You can now browse through Windows Server 2003's help files. You can install each edition's help and switch from one to another using the H&SC Options.

GS-22: Server Staging

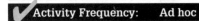

Activity Frequency:	Ad hoc

The size of the shop you are running and the number of servers within it will determine the frequency of this task. But some shops stage servers on a weekly basis if only to rebuild aging servers and redesign their service structure.

Server staging involves a lot of different activities. Windows Server 2003 also supports different server staging methods:

- **Manual or Interactive Staging** This method should be at least based on a thorough checklist.

- **Unattend Response File** This method is based on a rigorous and complete response file.

- **Disk Imaging with SysPrep** This method requires third-party disk image tools.

- **Remote Installation Services** This method builds a server from a model captured and stored on the RIS server.

- **Automated Deployment Services** This method combines RIS and disk imaging to provide the fastest and most accurate server construction process.

You should use ADS if at all possible—it is fast, can be used to create new machines as well as reconstruct them, and is easy to deploy.

TIP Information on the various installation methods and the preparation and management of reference servers can be found in Chapter 2 of Windows Server 2003: Best Practices for Enterprise Management, *by Ruest and Ruest (McGraw-Hill/Osborne, 2003).*

SCRIPT CENTER If you need to stage a vast number of servers at once, you can use a script from the Microsoft TechNet Script Center to automatically prestage the computer accounts required for each server at http:// www.microsoft.com/technet/treeview/ default.asp?url=/technet/scriptcenter/compmgmt/ ScrCM81.asp?frame=true.

---

*TIP It is a good idea to perform **Procedure HW-04** after a new server installation. This lets you identify any problematic devices.*

GS-23: Administrative Add-on Tool Setup

Activity Frequency: Ad hoc

There are several tools required to manage a Windows Server 2003 environment. These range from the basic Administrative Tool Pack to the Windows Server 2003 Support Tools and also include the Windows Server 2003 Resource Kit tools. Both the Administrative Tool Pack and the Support Tools can be found on the Windows Server installation CD (the first is in the C:\i386 folder and the second is in C:\Support\Tools). But all three can be downloaded from the Microsoft Download Web site. Just search for the tool kit name at www.microsoft.com/ downloads.

Installation of each tool kit is based on the Windows Installer service. Once downloaded, you can install them interactively or use **Procedure DC-15** to install them on target computers. You should install each set of tools on all servers and each administration machine.

 *Several tools in the Resource Kit grant high levels of privilege to users. Make sure you secure all tools properly through the use of Run As shortcuts (see **Procedure GS-01**).*

GS-24: Default User Profile Update

Activity Frequency: Ad hoc

There is nothing better than logging onto a system where everything is on hand for quick and easy management and administration. One of the best ways to do this is to customize an environment and copy this custom environment to the Default User profile. This way every new administrator that logs onto a server will have exactly the same tools on hand to manage the system.

Customization activities should include:

- Loading the Quick Launch Area with all of the shortcuts you use the most. This should include the Run As shortcuts you created in **Procedure GS-01**.

- Configure appropriate settings for the Windows Explorer (view all files, include the Status Bar, list items in detailed view).

- Install Administration, Support, and Resource Kit tools (see **Procedure GS-23**).

- It may even include the creation of a dummy administrator account with only Guest privileges for security purposes.

- It should definitely include the customization of desktop settings.

Once this is done, you can update the Default User profile so that it will always generate the same settings each time a new user profile is created.

 **SECURITY SCAN**   *The customization of desktop and other settings requires local administrative privileges.*

TIP   *You will need to create a second Administrator account to perform this activity. Use **Procedure GS-05** to do so. Windows Server 2003 does not allow you to copy an open user profile to another because many of the open features are volatile. To update your default user, you must use a second administrative account.*

To update the Default User profile:

1. Log out of Administrator (**Start Menu I Log Off**).

2. Log into your second administrative account. Windows Server creates a new profile based on old settings.

3. Open **Windows Explorer** (**Start Menu I All Programs I Accessories I Windows Explorer**) and set **Folder Options...** to view hidden files (**Tools I Folder Options I View** tab). Click **OK**.

4. Then, move to the left pane and right-click on **My Computer**.

5. Choose **User Profile Settings** under the **Advanced** tab.

6. Select the **Administrator** profile and click **Copy to**.

7. Browse to the **Documents and Settings** folder to find the **Default User** profile. Click **OK**.

8. Click **OK** to replace existing files.

9. Close all dialog boxes and **log out** of the second administrative account.

10. **Log** into Administrator.

11. Launch **Explorer** and return to the **User Profile** dialog box.

12. **Delete** the second administrative account's profile (it was created only to update Default User).

13. Close all dialog boxes and **log out** of the Administrator account.

14. Log into the second administrative account to test the **Default User**. Note that you now have a copy of the customized Administrator profile.

15. Return to the administrator profile.

TIP *You'll have to be careful with this operation when dealing with servers running Terminal Services because the Default User will be used to create user, not administrator, profiles. Obviously, user profiles will require different settings than administrative ones.*

GS-25: Technical Environment Review

Activity Frequency: **Ad hoc**

Once in a while, you should also take the time to review your entire technical environment and see if it requires any changes. This task is usually undertaken twice a year or during budget reviews. Use your activity logs and your troubleshooting reports to identify areas of improvement for your network and the services it delivers. You might also institute a user suggestion area. The best way to do this is to create a suggestion email alias and distribute it to users.

Document each proposed change in a business case to get funding and approval for the change. Carefully document each change you actually implement.

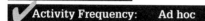

GS-26: System and Network Documentation

Activity Frequency: Ad hoc

You should also take the time to review your system and network documentation on an ad hoc basis. Is it up-to-date? Does it accurately describe your actual environment? This is not a task many of us relish as system administrators, but it is necessary nonetheless. Use appropriate tools such as Microsoft Office and Visio to perform your documentation.

In addition, Microsoft provides a series of tools that automatically document certain network aspects. These are the Microsoft Product Support's Customer Configuration Capture Tools and can be found by searching for their name at www.microsoft.com/download. Five tools are available to document Alliance (a special support program), Directory Services, Networking, Clustering, SUS, and Base Setup (includes File and Print Services and Performance).

Make sure your documentation is updated on a regular basis.

GS-27: Service Level Agreement Management

Activity Frequency: Ad hoc

Another ad hoc activity is the review of your service level agreements (SLAs). This should be done at least twice a year. SLAs refer to the agreements you enter into with your user community for the delivery of service. Services should be categorized according to priority, and different recovery times should be assigned to each priority. For example, a noncritical service can be restored in four hours or less while a critical service should be restored within one hour.

Once again, your troubleshooting reports will be highly useful during this review. User input is also highly valuable during this review because needs may change as users learn to better understand the capabilities of your systems.

GS-28: Troubleshooting Priority Management

✔**Activity Frequency:**   **Ad hoc**

Like **Procedure GS-27**, troubleshooting priority management should be reviewed twice a year. This review addresses how you should prioritize your activities when several different system problems occur. It is based on past performance and actual troubleshooting experience. It relies heavily on the SLAs you enter into with your user community.

Make sure you use an approach that is based on the least amount of effort for the greatest amount of benefit. For example, if a domain controller (DC) is down at the same time as a disk fails on the RAID 5 array of a file server, replace the disk first, then begin working at rebuilding the DC. This will be the most efficient way you can use your time. Use common sense to assign priorities.

GS-29: Workload Review

✔**Activity Frequency:**   **Ad hoc**

The final review you must perform on a biannual basis is the review of your workload. This *Pocket Administration Guide* helps you structure your days and weeks as an administrator. It also helps you automate a vast number of tasks through the use of automation and scripts.

You will still need to review your workload to make sure you have enough cycles to fulfill all tasks you should perform. If some tasks are not addressed at the frequency proposed

1

in this guide, you may require additional help. If so, carefully prepare a business case for your proposition and present it to your management. When such suggestions are well prepared and properly justified, they are rarely turned down.

Hardware Administration

All of the tasks included in hardware administration are placeholder tasks because even though it is vital that you perform them on a regular basis, it is difficult to document exactly how you must perform these tasks when there are so many different models and approaches to hardware management in the market.

Therefore, you will need to modify each task listed here to add your own customized activities.

HW-01: Network Hardware Checkup

Activity Frequency: **Weekly**

Your network is usually made up of a series of switches, hubs, routers, firewalls, and so on. Their continued good health will ensure the continued proper operation of Windows Server 2003. It is therefore useful that you take a regular walk through the computer room to review that network hardware is running properly. This includes the following activities:

- Looking over each of your network devices to make sure the proper indicator lights are turned on.

- Reviewing machine logs and configuration settings to make sure that a configuration is stable and to see if intrusions are occurring.

- Verifying cables and connections to make sure they are in good condition.

This task should be customized to include the tools supported by your environment.

HW-02: Server BIOS Management

✔ **Activity Frequency:**   Monthly

Like operating systems, BIOS versions continually change as manufacturers add capabilities and functionalities. Fortunately, most server manufacturers adhere to Desktop Management Task Force (www.dmtf.org) recommendations so that you no longer need to be sitting in front of a server to perform a BIOS upgrade. The tool you will use varies with the platform you are working with, but all major server manufacturers provide DMTF remote management tools. Intel even used to offer a generic DMTF remote management tool, LANDesk, that works with most Intel-based hardware. LANDesk is now available from LANDesk Software (www.landesksoftware.com). Whichever tool you use, you will often need to keep up-to-date BIOS and other hardware manufacturer software in order to fully qualify for ongoing support.

Once a month, you should review the availability of new BIOS editions for your hardware and check to see if you require the new BIOS in your environment. If so, download the new BIOS and use your DMTF tools to perform the upgrade on all targeted servers.

> *SCRIPT CENTER*   You can use a script from the Microsoft TechNet Script Center to retrieve system BIOS information. The script is available at http://www.microsoft.com/technet/treeview/default.asp?url=/technet/scriptcenter/compmgmt/ScrCM39.asp?frame=true.

HW-03: Firmware and Server Management Software Update Management

✔ **Activity Frequency:**   Monthly

In addition to BIOS software, hardware manufacturers provide both firmware and server management software. These tools support everything from telling you the status of the components inside your server cabinets to running specific hardware components. In most cases, these tools include a large number of different components. Therefore, they tend to be upgraded on a regular basis. Once again, you'll need to keep these up-to-date if you want continued support from your manufacturer.

Once a month, you should review the availability of new firmware and server management software editions for your hardware, and check to see if you require these new components in your environment. If so, download them and use your DMTF or server management software tools to perform the upgrade on all targeted servers.

HW-04: Device Management

Activity Frequency: **Ad hoc**

The way Windows Server 2003 interacts with hardware is through device drivers. The interface to these device drivers is the Device Manager, a component of the Computer Management MMC and now also a component of the Global MMC Console you created in **Procedure GS-17**.

Sometimes, drivers need to be updated or modified. In some instances, some devices may not work at all, especially if you use nonbrand-name servers (from clone manufacturers). Therefore it is at least worthwhile to verify that there are no device errors in the Device Manager.

To verify the status of device drivers:

1. Launch the **Global MMC Console** (**Quick Launch Area I Global MMC**).

2. Connect to the appropriate server (**Action I Connect to another computer**) and either type in the server name (\\servername) or use the **Browse** button to locate it. Click **OK** when done.

3. Select the **Device Manager** (**Computer Management I System Tools I Device Manager**).

4. View the status of your devices in the details pane. All devices should have closed trees. Any

problematic device will display an open tree and a yellow question mark.

5. Right-click on the problematic device to view its **Properties**. You can also use the context menu to select Update Driver. Identify the device's manufacturer and search for a new or updated driver. If no driver is available, deactivate the device.

 *Device drivers should be certified for Windows Server 2003 otherwise you cannot guarantee their stability. By default, Windows Server will warn you if you are installing a device that is not certified.*

Backup and Restore

Even though servers are designed to include redundancy systems for server and data protection, no organization could operate without a disaster recovery strategy that includes both a strong and regular backup strategy and a sound recovery system. The procedures outlined here are based on NTBackup.exe, the default backup tool included in Windows Server 2003. This edition of NTBackup is much more complete than previous editions, with the addition of both the Volume Shadow Copy service and the Automated Systems Recovery option. The first lets the system take a snapshot of all data before taking the backup, resolving many issues with the backup of open files. The second lets you rebuild a server without having to reinstall its software.

But if your enterprise is serious about its data, you will most likely have a more comprehensive backup engine. The best of these is QiNetix from Commvault Systems Inc. (www.commvault.com). This is the only backup tool that fully supports Active Directory, letting you restore objects and attributes directly within the directory without having to perform an authoritative restore—an operation that is rather complex. In addition, if you have massive volumes of data, QiNetix will save you considerable time—especially for full backups because it builds a full backup image from past incremental backups, using a unique single-instance store technology. This means that you never run out of time to do your backup because it isn't actually drawn from the systems themselves, but rather from previous backup images.

BR-01: System State Backup Generation

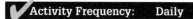

Activity Frequency: **Daily**

System state backups are critical on each server because these are the tools that protect the operating system itself. There are nine potential elements to a system state backup. Some are always backed up and others depend on the type of server you are backing up. They are identified as follows:

- The system registry
- The COM+ Class registry database
- Boot and system files
- Windows file protection system files
- Active Directory database (on domain controllers)
- SYSVOL Directory (on domain controllers)
- Certificate Services database (on certificate servers)
- Cluster service configuration information (on server clusters)
- IIS Metadirectory (on Web application servers)

System state data is always backed up as a whole and cannot be segregated. This is a daily task that should be automated. To schedule a system state backup:

1. Use the **Global MMC Console** to open a **Remote Desktop Connection** (see **Procedure RA-01**) to the server you want to verify. Launch **NTBackup** (**Quick Launch Area | Backup**). Make sure it launches in **Advanced** mode.

2. Move to the **Scheduled Jobs** tab and click **Add Job**.

3. This launches the Backup Wizard to let you define the parameters of the Job. Click **Next**.

4. Select **Only backup the System State data** and click **Next**.

5. Identify the backup location. This should be on removable media. Click **Next**.

6. Check **Verify data after backup** and **Use Hardware compression, if available** and click **Next**. Do not disable volume shadow copy.

7. Select to **Append** the data or **Replace** backups and click **Next**.

8. Name the job and click **Set Schedule** to identify a **Weekly** schedule (Monday to Friday). Click **OK** when done. Identify the account to run the backup under and click **OK**. Click **Next**. Click **Finish** to close the wizard.

Repeat the procedure to create data backups on the same schedule and add full backups on weekends.

BR-02: Backup Verification

 Activity Frequency: Daily

Even though backups are a lot easier to do and more reliable with WS03, you should still take the time to make sure they have been properly performed. To do so, you need to view the backup log on each file server. To check backup logs:

1. Use the **Global MMC Console** to open a **Remote Desktop Connection** to the server you want to verify.

2. Launch the **Backup** tool in **Advanced View** (**Quick Launch Area | Backup**).

3. Use **Tool | Report** to view reports.

4. Select the appropriate report from the Backup Reports dialog box and click on **View**.

5. Search for the word **Error** in the report log.

If you find errors, determine if it is a critical file and use the Windows Explorer to see why the file wasn't backed up or if it needs to be recovered. Make note of the results of your investigation in your Daily Activity Log (**Procedure GS-06**).

BR-03: Off-site Storage Tape Management

Activity Frequency: Weekly

One of the key elements of a disaster recovery strategy is the protection of your backup tapes. After all, if your data center burns down and all your backup tapes burn with it, it will be rather hard for you to reconstruct your systems. Therefore, you should make sure that you store your weekly backup tapes in at a different site. This site should be protected from disasters. This can be anything from a safety deposit box in a bank to a specialized data protection service.

This means that once a week you should take your full weekend backup and send it off site to a protected vault and recover older backups to reuse the tapes. You should also consider keeping a full monthly backup off site as well as at least one yearly backup (this can be the monthly backup for the last month in your fiscal year).

BR-04: Disaster Recovery Strategy Testing

Activity Frequency: Monthly

A disaster recovery strategy is only as good as its proven ability to recover and reconstruct your systems. Therefore, you should take the time to validate your disaster recovery strategy on a monthly basis. This means making sure that everything that makes up the disaster recovery strategy is in place and ready to support your system reconstruction at any time. This includes having spare parts, spare servers, spare network components, off-site storage of backup tapes, a sound backup tape rotation system, regular tape drive cleaning processes, documented procedures for system reconstruction (especially AD reconstruction), and so on. This review should be based on a checklist that you use to validate each of the elements that support system recovery. Document any changes you bring to this strategy after you complete the review.

You should also run an automated system recovery (ASR) backup job on each of your servers. The ASR backup is run manually because it creates a recovery diskette. It should be run once a month to make sure the ASR diskette is up-to-date. It should also be run whenever you make significant changes to any server. ASR captures system state, installed services, all information about the disks installed in the system, and how to restore the server. To run an ASR backup:

1. Use the **Global MMC Console** to open a **Remote Desktop Connection** to the server you want to verify. Launch **NTBackup** (**Quick Launch Area** | **Backup**). Make sure it launches in **Advanced** mode.

2. In the Backup Welcome screen, click **Automated System Recovery**. This launches the ASR Wizard. Click **Next**.

3. Select the type and the name of the backup, then click **Next**.

4. Click **Finish** to begin the ASR backup. Make sure you have a diskette on hand to create the ASR boot disk.

Store your ASR disks in a safe place.

TIP *The ASR backup is not a complete system backup. It is only used to rebuild the operating system. Make sure you complete the system protection process with a complete data backup.*

BR-05: Restore Procedure Testing

Activity Frequency: Monthly

Backups are only as good as their ability to restore information to a system. Therefore, once a month you

should perform a restore test from a random copy of your
backup media to make sure it actually works. Too many
organizations have been caught empty-handed when they
tried to restore critical files from backup tapes that were
never tested only to find out that they didn't work. To test
the restore procedure:

1. Select a backup media at random and insert it into a
   server drive.

2. Use the **Global MMC Console** to open a **Remote
   Desktop Connection** to the server you want to
   verify. Launch **NTBackup (Quick Launch Area |
   Backup**). Make sure it launches in **Advanced** mode.

3. In the Backup Welcome screen, click **Restore Wizard**.
   This launches the Restore Wizard. Click **Next**.

4. Select the backup to restore from or click **Browse** to
   locate it.

5. Expand the backup listing to identify a random file
   to restore. Click **Next**.

6. Click the **Advanced** button to restore the file to a
   new, test location.

7. Click **Finish** to begin the restore.

Verify the integrity of the files you restore. Destroy the
files when done.

BR-06: Backup Strategy Review

Activity Frequency: **Monthly**

Once a month you should also take the time to review your
backup strategy. Has the volume of backups changed? Is
there new information to include into your backups? Is
your backup schedule appropriate? These and other
questions should help you form a checklist that you can
use to review your backup strategy.

Document any changes you make.

BR-07: Server Rebuild

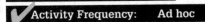

Activity Frequency: Ad hoc

Once in a while, you should also take the time to test your server rebuild process. This means taking a test server, crashing it by destroying a RAID array, and performing a complete rebuild using your automated systems recovery backup and diskette. This test should be performed at least twice a year.

To rebuild a server using ASR:

1. Use your Windows Server 2003 installation CD to launch System Setup. Press F2 when prompted and insert the ASR floppy. Make sure your backup media is also available and online.

2. ASR Restore will restore the disk signatures, install a minimal version of Windows, and restore all system files.

3. Once the ASR restore is complete, restore data files from data backups.

4. Verify the server completely, making sure it is fully functional.

Document any changes you make to your ASR recovery procedure.

Remote Administration

Windows 2000 introduced the concept of remote server administration through Terminal Services in Administration Mode. This allows you to make up to two remote connections to a server without additional Terminal Services client licenses. In Windows Server 2003, this feature has been renamed to match the same feature in Windows XP. It is now called Remote Desktop Connections (RDC).

RDC is a boon to server administrators because it gives you complete access to a server's desktop without having to access the server physically.

 **SECURITY SCAN** *RDC is secure because it limits access to server rooms. Administrators can work from their own desks to administer and configure servers remotely.*

RA-01: Server RDC Management

 **Activity Frequency:** **Monthly**

Once a month, you should review your remote server management practices. This review should serve to answer such questions as: Are our remote connections secure? How many administrators have remote access to servers? Do we change our administrative passwords frequently enough? Are the consoles that give remote access to servers sufficiently protected?

TIP *Remember that Remote Desktop Connections are only required if you need to modify settings on a server. Try to make a habit of working with the Global MMC Console instead.*

Remote Desktop Connections can only occur if the **Remote Desktop** setting has been enabled on the server. To enable this setting:

1. Launch the **System Properties** dialog box (**Start Menu | Control Panel | System**).

2. Move to the **Remote** tab and check **Allow users to connect remotely to this computer**.

3. You do not need to do anything else if your administrators are all members of the local Administrators group because they automatically have access to the server. Alternatively, you can add remote server operators to the **Remote Desktop Users** built-in group (**Active Directory Users and Computers | Built-in**). This will give them access

to the local desktop in a remote session. If they are not members of either group, you must enumerate the users one by one. Click on **Select Remote Users** to do so.

4. Click **OK** in each dialog box when done.

You can also set this option remotely through Group Policy. Use **Procedure DC-16** to edit the appropriate GPO. This should be a GPO that applies to servers only. Enable the setting **Allow users to connect remotely using Terminal Services** (**Computer Configuration | Administrative Template | Terminal Services**). This GPO setting provides the same functionality as the checkbox in System Properties.

Now that your servers will allow remote connections, you need to create an actual connection to each server. Use the Global MMC Console created in **Procedure GS-17**.

1. Move to **Remote Desktops** (**Computer Management | Remote Desktops**).

2. Right-click on **Remote Desktops** and select **Add new connection**.

3. Type in the DNS name of the server, name the connection, make sure **Connect to console** is checked, and type in the credentials (User Name, Password, and Domain). Check **Save password** to create an auto-logon connection. Click **OK** when done. Repeat for each server.

SECURITY SCAN *Be sure you have secured your Global MMC Console through a Run As Shortcut (**Procedure GS-01**) if you choose to create an auto-logon connection because this can be a major security risk.*

From now on, when you need to connect to a server, all you have to do is click its connection name once. Right-click on the connection name to select **Disconnect** when you're done.

TIP *RDC in Administration Mode allows two
connections at once. The best practice is to identify
immediately upon connection whether someone else is
working on the server at the same time. The best way to
do this is to open a Command Console and type* **query
user**. *If another administrator is logged on, contact this
administrator to make sure you will not both be
performing conflicting activities on the same server.*

RA-02: PC RDC Management

Activity Frequency: **Monthly**

PC RDC management is the same as for servers and uses
exactly the same approach (see **Procedure RA-01**). But
since you tend to have many more desktops than servers,
it is a good idea to create a single PC management
console. To do so:

1. Use **Procedure GS-17** to create an new console, but
   this time run the mmc command as follows:

   mmc /a

2. This opens an empty Microsoft Management
   Console. Add the **Remote Desktop** snap-in to the
   console root.

3. Save the console as **PC Management** in the
   C:\Toolkit folder. Make sure it is a console that can
   be modified during use. Close the console.

4. Launch it again by clicking on the console name.
   Add a new connection to each PC you manage.

5. **Save** the console (**File | Save**).

Make sure all PCs are managed by a GPO that enables
Remote Desktop Connections. Secure this console through
a Run As Shortcut (**Procedure GS-01**).

TIP *PCs only allow a single logon at a time. If you log on
remotely to a PC while a user is already logged on, the user
will be logged off automatically. If you need to provide
assistance to a user, use* **Procedure RA-03** *instead.*

RA-03: User Support through Remote Assistance

Activity Frequency: Ad hoc

If you need to provide remote support to a user, especially while the user is still logged on, you cannot use a Remote Desktop Connection because it automatically logs off the user. Use Remote Assistance instead.

Remote Assistance works in one of two ways. It can let users request assistance from the Help Desk or it can let Help Desk operators offer assistance to users. Users must explicitly accept assistance before either can proceed. Remote Assistance is controlled through two GPO settings: **Solicited Remote Assistance** and **Offer Remote Assistance** (**Computer Configuration | Administrative Templates | System | Remote Assistance**). Each includes the ability to identify **Helpers** in your organization. Solicited RA lets you also set both the times during which users can request assistance and the request mechanism (mailto or Simple MAPI). In addition, each lets you determine the type of assistance to offer, identifying whether support personnel can interact with the desktop or simply watch. Interaction provides the fullest support but can represent a security risk.

SECURITY SCAN *Remember that before a Helper can assist a user or interact with their desktop, users must first accept the offer for remote assistance. Be sure to warn users never to leave their desktops unattended while someone else is interacting with it.*

Both require a list of helpers. Helpers are user groups that are typed in the format *domainname\groupname*.

TIP *These GPO settings do not let you select group names from AD; you must type them in manually. Be sure to verify the information you typed in before applying these GPO settings to your PCs.*

Once these settings are applied to all PCs, you can offer
help in the following manner:

1. Launch **Help and Support Center (Quick Launch
   Area | Help and Support)**.

2. Click **Tools (Support Tasks | Tools)**.

3. Expand **Help and Support Tools** in the left pane and
   click **Offer Remote Assistance**.

4. Type the DNS name of the PC you want to connect
   to and click **Connect**.

5. Wait for the user to accept the connection before
   beginning your support.

This task is set as an ad hoc task because, hopefully, you
will not need to perform it on a regular basis.

RA-04: Remote Desktop Connection
Shortcut and Web Access

 **Activity Frequency: Ad hoc**

Since you have created a Global MMC Console (see
Procedure GS-17) that includes the Remote Connection
snap-in, you should have very little need for RDC Shortcuts.
The console provides much simpler connectivity than
individual shortcuts would. But you might find that you
need to connect to a server remotely when you are away
from your desk. The best way to do this is to publish the
Remote Desktop Connection Web page and use it to
remotely connect to servers from any desktop.

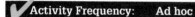 **SECURITY SCAN** *Make sure you never forget to close
Remote Desktop Connections to
servers once you're done connecting from a computer not
your own.*

The Remote Desktop Web Client (RDWC) is not installed
by default. You need to perform this operation on a server
hosting Internet Information Server (IIS). If not, you will
need to install IIS on a server. Use the following procedure

to install it. The Windows Server 2003 installation CD is required for this operation.

1. Launch **Add or Remove Programs (Start Menu | Control Panel)** and select **Add/Remove Windows Components**.

2. Move to **Web Application Server** and click **Details**.

3. Move to **Internet Information Server** and click **Details**.

4. Move to **World Wide Web Service** and click **Details**.

5. Select **Remote Desktop Web Connection** and click **OK**. Click **OK** three times to return to the Web Components dialog box. Click **Next**.

6. Once the client is installed, you can move to the %SystemRoot%\Web\TSWeb folder and open Default.htm to view the default RDWC page.

7. This page can be edited to meet your corporate standards and placed on your intranet to give administrators remote access to servers through a web interface.

TIP *You must modify the default Internet Explorer security settings on the server; otherwise, users will not be able to properly view this page. Use **Tools | Internet Options | Security** in Internet Explorer to set the **Local Intranet** zone to **Default Level**. This should allow users to automatically download the Terminal Services ActiveX control located on this page.*

Once done, you can use this page to access all your servers from any PC.

Chapter 2

Administering File and Print Servers

File and print servers are sometimes the very reason organizations implement networks. For this reason, they are also often the very first servers to be put in place in a networked system. This is why they are the first specific server role examined in this book.

Administrative Activities

The administration of file and print servers is divided into three categories. These include File Services, Print Services and Cluster Services. Table 2-1 outlines the administrative activities that you must perform on an ongoing basis to ensure proper operation of the services you deliver to your user community. It also identifies the frequency of each task.

Procedure Number	Activity	Frequency
File Services		
FS-01	Available Free Space Verification	Daily
FS-02	Data Backup Management	Daily
FS-03	Shared Folder Management	Daily
FS-04	File Replication Service Event Log Verification	Daily
FS-05	Volume Shadow Copy Management	Weekly
FS-06	Distributed File System Management	Weekly
FS-07	Quota Management	Weekly
FS-08	Indexing Service Management	Weekly

Table 2-1. File and Print Service Administration Task List

Procedure Number	Activity	Frequency
FS-09	Data Disk Integrity Verification	Weekly
FS-10	Data Disk Defragmentation	Weekly
FS-11	File Access Audit Log Verification	Weekly
FS-12	Temporary File Cleanup	Weekly
FS-13	Security Parameter Verification	Weekly
FS-14	Encrypted Folder Management	Weekly
FS-15	Data Archiving	Monthly
FS-16	File Replication Service Management	Monthly
FS-17	Disk and Volume Management	Ad hoc
Print Services		
PS-01	Print Queue Management	Daily
PS-02	Printer Access Management	Weekly
PS-03	Printer Driver Management	Weekly
PS-04	Printer Sharing	Ad hoc
PS-05	Print Spooler Drive Management	Ad hoc
PS-06	Printer Location Tracking Management	Ad hoc
PS-07	Massive Printer Management	Ad hoc
PS-08	New Printer Model Evaluation	Ad hoc
Cluster Services		
CS-01	Clusters: Cluster State Verification	Daily
CS-02	Clusters: Print Queue Status Verification	Daily
CS-03	Clusters: Server Cluster Management	Weekly
CS-04	Clusters: Quorum State Verification	Weekly

Table 2-1. File and Print Service Administration Task List
(continued)

You may not need to perform all of these activities because you don't use some of the services mentioned here. You may also use a different schedule. Remember to personalize the task list to adapt it to your environment.

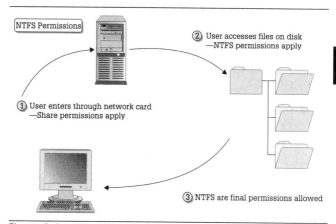

Figure 2-1. The file access security process

 *You should modify security settings on root folders because* these settings are inherited whenever you create subfolders. This way, you will only need to fine-tune subfolder settings from then on.

You can share folders in three ways: the *Windows Explorer*, the *File Server Management* console or the net share command. To share folders with the Explorer (since you just used it to create a folder):

1. Locate the folder you want —to share, right-click on it and select **Sharing**.

2. Identify the **name for the share**—if possible, the name of the folder—and type in a **description**.

3. Now set share permissions. If you set NTFS permissions properly, you can set share permissions to **Authenticated Users: Change**. Do so by clicking **Add**, locating **Authenticated Users** and checking the **Change** setting. Remove **Everyone** from the share security settings. Close the dialog box.

 *Remember that, by default, all shares are set to **Everyone: Read**.* *It is important to verify security settings every time you create a new shared folder.*

4. Next, set **Offline Settings**. By default all shares are set to allow users to determine if they want offline copies. Use the **Offline Settings** button to select the appropriate setting for this share.

5. Click **OK** when done. Repeat for each new share.

You're almost done. Now, the only thing left is to make the shares available to users. This is done through Active Directory.

To publish a share in Active Directory:

1. Open a Remote Desktop Connection on a **domain controller** and open the **Active Directory Users and Computers** console.

2. Locate the organizational unit you want to use to publish shared folders or create a **new organizational unit** and name it appropriately.

3. Now, move to the right pane and right-click to select **New, Shared Folder** from the context menu.

4. Type in the **name of the share** and the **path to the shared folder** (using Universal Naming Convention format or \\servername\sharename). Click **OK** when done. Repeat for each share you need to publish.

Once the shares are created, you will need to add a description and keywords to each. Folder descriptions are useful since they will help users identify the purpose of the shared folder. Keywords are also useful because users can search for shared folders by keyword instead of share name.

1. To enter both, view the **Properties** of each shared folder in AD.

2. Add complete descriptions to each share and identify its **Manager**.

3. To add keywords, click the **Keywords** button. Type the **keyword** and click **Add.** Click **OK** when done.

4. Close the dialog box when done. Repeat for each share you publish in AD.

2

TIP *Do not publish hidden shares (using the Share$ name format) because they will no longer be hidden. Any share that is published in AD will be visible to users.*

Your shares are now ready for access by users.

FS-04: File Replication Service Event Log Verification

Activity Frequency: **Daily**

The File Replication Service (FRS) is at the core of both the Distributed File System and Active Directory operations. Its proper operation must be verified daily. The best way to do this is to use the Global MMC Console you created in **Procedure GS-17** and follow much the same steps as outlined in **Procedure GS-03**.

1. Launch the **Global MMC Console** (**Quick Launch Area | Global MMC Console**).

2. Connect to the appropriate server (**Action | Connect to another computer**) and either type in the server name (\\servername) or use the **Browse** button to locate it. Click **OK** when done.

3. Move to the **FRS Event Log** (**System Tools | Event Viewer | File Replication Service**).

4. Identify any errors or warnings. Take appropriate action if either appears.

Make note of any corrective action you need to take. Use **Procedure GS-06** to log the different events you investigate each day.

FS-05: Volume Shadow Copy Management

Activity Frequency: Weekly

The Volume Shadow Copy service (VSC) is a very useful tool for system administrators because it provides users with the ability to restore their own files. It also provides the ability to create backups from copies or snapshots of production data letting you back up data without affecting production environments.

Shadow copies are a feature of disk drives. To verify the status of VSC:

1. Use the **Global MMC Console** to open a **Remote Desktop Connection** to the appropriate server and then open the **Windows Explorer (Quick Launch Area | Windows Explorer)**.

2. Navigate to the data drive (drive D:) and right-click on it to select **Properties**.

3. Move to the **Shadow Copies** tab and click **Settings**.

4. In the Settings dialog box, click **Details**. This will display a dialog box outlining the volume shadow copies are located on, the amount of available space on the volume, and the amount of space used by VSC. Verify that enough space is available for the shadow copies and click **OK** to close the dialog box.

TIP   *Shadow copies should be located on a dedicated volume. This makes sure the VSC service does not interfere with production service levels.*

5. Verify the **Maximum size** allocated to the VSC service and modify it if required.

6. You should also check the VSC schedule. Click **Schedule**, verify that everything is as it should be and click **OK** when done. The default schedule is usually appropriate for most environments.

2

7. Close the **Properties** dialog box when done, by clicking **OK**.

You should make sure that VSC Restores work properly. To verify VSC restores:

1. On your own computer, launch the **Windows Explorer (Quick Launch Area | Windows Explorer)**.

2. Locate a shared folder you have access to and select a test file within this folder. Right-click on it to view its **Properties**.

3. Move to the **Previous Versions** tab and select the version of the file you want to restore and click **Restore**. It will give you a warning about overwriting newer versions. Click **OK** to proceed.

4. Close the Properties dialog box when done.

The file should be located in the folder you selected. While VSC does not replace backups, it offers user self-service for short-term file recoveries.

TIP *To be able to access previous versions of files, you must have deployed the Previous Versions Client to Windows XP PCs. The Previous Versions client is a Windows Installer file named TWCLI32.MSI. It is located in the %SystemRoot%\System32\Clients folder. Locate the appropriate version (32 or 64-bit) and deploy it to all users of Windows XP machines. In fact, it should be part of the basic build of all client systems.*

You can also use the `vssadmin` command-line tool to manage Volume Shadow Copies. For example, to list the shadow copies currently on a volume, type:

```
vssadmin list shadows
```

You can also pipe this command to a text file to capture the information more rapidly. The `vssadmin` command is very useful. It lists shadow copies, lists volumes eligible for shadow copies, creates and deletes shadow copies and more. For more information, simply type `vssadmin` at the command prompt.

FS-06: Distributed File System Management

✔ Activity Frequency: Weekly

The Distributed File System (DFS) is one of Windows Server 2003's most powerful file services. It provides fully redundant file share access in either stand-alone or domain-based mode. Figure 2-2 illustrates the DFS creation process in either mode.

Use the DFS console to ensure the proper operation of this service.

1. Launch the **DFS console** (**Start Menu | Administrative Tools | Distributed File System**).

2. If the DFS root you want to manage is not visible, use the Action menu to connect to your DFS roots (**Action | Show Root**), locate the root you want to manage, select it and click **OK**.

3. To make sure the DFS share is operating properly, right-click on the **DFS share name** and select **Check status** from the context menu.

4. All root targets should show a status of *online*. If not, verify why the targets are not online and repair them (the server may be down).

TIP   *DFS depends heavily on the Remote Procedure Call service. Make sure this service is up and running. Also, domain-based DFS roots must have synchronized clocks (to support replication and location of the root targets). Make sure all systems are synchronized with the PDC Emulator (this is normally the default in an Active Directory domain).*

The DFS console can also be used to modify the DFS configuration, add new targets, add new links, configure replication and so on.

Stand-alone DFS roots tend to be applied more often in server clusters. If you use server clusters and stand-alone

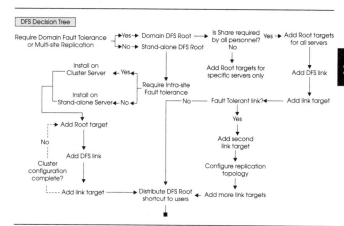

Figure 2-2. The DFS creation process

DFS roots, you will have the opportunity to reuse this procedure.

SCRIPT CENTER *The Microsoft TechNet Script Center includes several scripts that help you identify work with DFS. These scripts can be found at http:// www.microsoft.com/technet/treeview/default.asp?url=/ technet/scriptcenter/dfs/default.asp?frame=true.*

FS-07: Quota Management

Activity Frequency: **Weekly**

The Windows Server 2003 Quota Service is also a feature of disk drives. To verify quota status:

1. Use the **Global MMC Console** to open a **Remote Desktop Connection** to the appropriate server and then open the **Windows Explorer** (**Quick Launch Area | Windows Explorer**).

2. Navigate to the data drive (drive D:) and right-click on it to select **Properties**.

3. Move to the **Quota** tab and click **Quota Entries**.

4. View all quota entries and verify how your users are making use of shared disk space.

5. You can view a user's individual settings by right-clicking on the user and selecting **Properties**. Close the Quota Entries window when done.

You can also import quota settings from another volume. If you need to do so (replacing a volume, moving data to a new volume), make sure you export the settings (**Quota | Export**) from the source volume before you import them (**Quota | Import**) into the destination volume.

SCRIPT CENTER   *The Microsoft TechNet Script Center includes several scripts that help you identify work with quotas. These scripts can be found at http://www.microsoft.com/technet/treeview/default.asp?url=/technet/scriptcenter/dfs/default.asp?frame=true.*

FS-08: Indexing Service Management

Activity Frequency: Weekly

The WS03 Indexing Service will index documents in the following formats:

- Text, HTML, Office 95 and later, Internet Mail and News, and any other document for which a filter is available

For example, Adobe Corporation provides an indexing filter for documents in the PDF format. This filter can be found at http://download.adobe.com/pub/adobe/acrobat/win/all/ifilter50.exe.

In addition each drive must be marked for indexing and the Indexing Service must be turned on. Drive marking is performed in the **Properties** dialog box for the drive under the **General** tab. This setting is turned on by default on all drives. Since data is located only on specific drives, you should uncheck it for system drives.

To verify that the Indexing Service is turned on, use the Global MMC Console (**Procedure GS-17**) to view the service status (**Services and Applications | Services**). Make sure it is set to automatic startup.

To verify that the Indexing Service is working properly, search for a document you know is on the drive (**Start Menu | Search**).

2

FS-09: Data Disk Integrity Verification

Activity Frequency: **Weekly**

Because data is stored on drives and drives tend to be the major point of failure on any given system, it is important to verify that the volumes you use are regularly scanned for integrity.

To scan a disk for integrity, use the following command:

```
chkdsk volume: /f
```

where *volume:* is the name of the drive or volume you want checked. This command can be set as a **Scheduled Task** (see **Procedure GS-19**).

You can also perform this command through the graphical interface. Use **Windows Explorer** to locate the disk drive you want to verify, right-click on it, select **Properties**, move to the **Tools** tab and click **Check Now**.

TIP   *This command can only be run in real-time on nonsystem volumes. Since CheckDisk needs exclusive access to a volume during verification, it can only run at server startup on system volumes.*

SCRIPT CENTER   *The Microsoft TechNet Script Center includes two scripts that help you work with disk verifications. The first lets you run Chkdsk on a volume and the second tells you the status of Chkdks on a volume. These scripts can be found at http:// www.microsoft.com/ technet/treeview/default.asp?url=/ technet/scriptcenter/dfs/ScrDFS34.asp?frame=true and http:// www.microsoft.com/technet/treeview/ default.asp?url=/technet/scriptcenter/dfs/ scrdfs36.asp?frame=true.*

FS-10: Data Disk Defragmentation

✔ Activity Frequency: **Weekly**

It is also important to defragment drives on a regular basis to improve performance and data access speeds.

To defragment a disk, use the following command:

```
defrag volume /v >filename.txt
```

where *volume* is the name of the drive or volume you want to defragment. Using the /v switch enables the verbose mode which can be piped into the file of your choice. This command can also be set as a **Scheduled Task** (see **Procedure GS-19**).

You can also perform this command through the graphical interface. Use **Windows Explorer** to locate the disk drive you want to verify, right-click on it, select **Properties**, move to the **Tools** tab and click **Defragment Now**.

FS-11: File Access Audit Log Verification

✔ Activity Frequency: **Weekly**

SECURITY SCAN *One of the foremost responsibilities of a file system administrator is to make sure people access only those files they are allowed to. Therefore it is essential to enable file access auditing on data drives, especially if the data is either sensitive, confidential or secret.*

File access auditing is enabled through Group Policy and must be specifically applied to the objects you want to audit. Use the following procedure:

1. Use the **Global MMC Console** to view the **Group Policy Management Console** (**Start Menu | Global MMC Console**).

2. Move to the **Group Policy Object** container (**GPMC | Forest | Domains | Domainname | Group Policy Objects**) and locate the GPO you want to modify. This policy may apply at the domain level or could

be focused on an organizational unit that stores all of the file servers. Right-click on the policy and select **Edit**.

3. Turn on the object access audit policy (**Computer Configuration I Windows Settings I Security Settings I Local Policy I Audit Policy**).

4. Next you must identify the folders you want to audit (**Computer Configuration I Windows Settings I Security Settings I File System**). To do so, you must use the **Add file** command, locate the folder you want to audit, click the **Advanced** button, move to the **Audit** tab, click **Add**, locate the group you want to audit (Everyone), and identify the events you want to audit for this group.

 *This is one of the rare opportunities where the Everyone group applies, because in fact you do not want to audit only Authenticated Users, but everyone who has access to the system.*

5. Close all dialog boxes and the Group Policy Editor when done.

6. Use the **Global MMC Console** to view the results of the audit under **System Tools I Event Viewer I Security**.

*TIP Auditing object access creates a lot of entries. Be careful what you choose to audit and make sure your Security Event Log is set to an appropriate file size (**System Tools I Event Viewer I Security I Properties**).*

FS-12: Temporary File Cleanup

Applications need to create temporary files to ensure that users do not lose their data as they work. These temporary files are normally removed when the application closes. Unfortunately, not all applications are so well behaved.

Thus, you must verify data disks for temporary or corrupt files to delete them on a regular basis.

You can do this interactively using the Disk Cleanup utility. Use the following procedure to do so:

1. Launch **Disk Cleanup** (**Start Menu** | **All Programs** | **Accessories** | **System Tools** | **Disk Cleanup**).

2. Select the disk you want to clean up and click **OK**. (No disk selection is offered when the system has only one drive.) Disk Cleanup scans the computer for files that can be deleted.

3. Select the files to clean up or compress and click **OK**.

4. Click **Yes** to confirm the operation.

You can also do this by creating a global script that regularly scans drives and removes all temporary or corrupt files. This script should be run at times when few users are logged on even though it will operate properly when users have active temporary files on the volume because active files are locked and cannot be deleted.

The script should delete the following file types:

- *.tmp
- ~*.*

Use the following commands in your script:

```
del volume:*.tmp /s /q >filename.txt
del volume:~*.* /s /q /a:h >filename.txt
```

where *volume:* is the name of the data drive. The /s and /q switches respectively mean including files located in subdirectories and don't ask for confirmation and the /a:h switch ensures that you delete only temporary files because they are normally hidden from users (some users may use the tilde (~) in their filenames). Finally, piping the information into a file (*filename.txt*) gives you a complete listing of all deleted files.

FS-13: Security Parameter Verification

Activity Frequency: **Weekly**

2

SECURITY SCAN *Security is always a concern in a networked data environment. Therefore, it is necessary to verify that security settings are appropriate on data and system drives.*

The best way to verify security settings is to use the Security Configuration Manager in analysis mode. It compares an existing security implementation to a baseline security template and outlines the differences. This means that you must keep track of all the changes you make to security settings on data drives and you must update your baseline security template on a regular basis.

To analyze a computer and compare it to a given security policy in graphical mode, use **Procedure GS-20**. If you need to perform this verification on several systems, you should do so via a command line. The command to use is:

```
secedit /analyze /db filename.sdb /log filename.log
```

In addition, the /verbose switch can be used to create a log file that is highly detailed. If no log file is specified, secedit will automatically log all information to the scesrv.log file in the %windir%\security\logs folder. To configure a computer instead of analyzing it, replace the /analyze switch with /configure.

TIP This command must be run locally. If you create scripts to run this command, make sure you design them to run locally on each file server.

SECURITY SCAN *You can also verify and modify file and folder security settings with the cacls and xcacls commands. These commands are very useful for adding and removing security descriptors to and from files and folders without modifying existing security parameters. Use the /? switch with both commands for more information.*

FS-14: Encrypted Folder Management

Activity Frequency: Weekly

SECURITY SCAN *File encryption is used to protect confidential information. Shared folder encryption is new to WS03.*

To encrypt data in shared folders, the file servers must be trusted for delegation within Active Directory. This is a property of the server's computer account within the directory (**Server Name | Properties | Delegation | Trust this computer for delegation to any service (Kerberos only)**).

In addition, folders can only contain one of two values: compression or encryption. If a folder is not available for encryption, it is because its compression value is set.

Finally, encryption settings are applied through a folder's properties (**Properties | General tab | Advanced**) and encrypted files and folders are displayed in green in the Windows Explorer.

FS-15: Data Archiving

Activity Frequency: Monthly

Windows Server 2003 does not really include any special tool for archiving data, though it does include support for archival technology such as remote offline storage. You can use NT Backup to perform a backup of selected data for archival purposes, then remove the data from the network to create additional free space, but this is not necessarily an easy task. To archive data based on creation/modification date in Windows Server 2003, you must launch **Windows Backup** (**Start Menu | All Programs | Accessories | Backup**), move to the **Backup** tab, expand your data disk in the selection window, view each of the folders in the drive and sort files by date (click on the **Modified** title in the right pane) and select all of the oldest files, then run the backup. You'll also need to print the backup report to identify which files to delete.

It is much simpler to create special archive-shared folders and ask users to place data that can be archived into these special shares. Then, on a regular basis, back them up and delete the folder's contents.

2

FS-16: File Replication Service Management

 **Activity Frequency:** **Monthly**

Procedure FS-04 identifies that you must regularly check the FRS Event Log to make sure there are no replication errors. You also have to make sure the FRS replication rules are set properly and meet your network configuration's capabilities for replication, though this is done less often.

The items to verify are the following:

- Replication topology and schedule

- Files excluded from replication and replication priority

FRS is managed from the DFS console (Start Menu | Administrative Tools | Distributed File System).

1. If you don't see your DFS roots, use the **Action** menu to connect to them (**Action | Show Root**), and then locate the root you want to manage, select it and click **OK**.

2. Expand the DFS share name in the left pane to display the DFS links. Right-click on a link and select **Show replication information**.

3. Review the replication status for each DFS link.

FRS uses four different replication topologies: ring, hub and spoke, full mesh, and custom. You can change the replication mode by right-clicking on the DFS share name and selecting **Configure replication**.

TIP *FRS supports automatic replication on domain-based DFS roots. To do so, it requires a staging folder where it stores temporary files. You should also verify that the disk hosting this folder (FRS-Staging) has enough space to support the automatic replication process. You can use* **Procedure FS-01** *to do so.*

In addition, you can use SONAR, a Resource Kit tool that is designed to monitor both FRS Replica Set members and their status. SONAR runs as a command-line tool. It must first be installed on a system:

1. Locate **SONAR.exe** on the Resource Kit CD (or search for SONAR at www.microsoft.com/download) and use the following command:

   ```
   sonar /i
   ```

2. Once SONAR is installed, all you need to do is start it:

   ```
   sonar /s
   ```

3. This opens a dialog box that lets you select the **Domain**, and the **Replica Set**, and the Refresh Rate, and identify if you want to view only Hub data or all data.

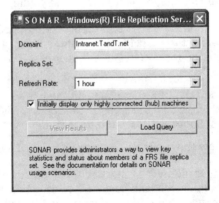

4. To view the results, click **View Results**.

5. To stop SONAR, use **File | Exit**. **Save** your changes if you have made any.

Alternatively, you can store all the parameters in a file and launch SONAR with the configuration stored in this file. Type `sonar /?` for more information.

SCRIPT CENTER *The Microsoft TechNet Script Center includes a script that helps you monitor FRS replication. This script can be found at http:// www.microsoft.com/ technet/treeview/default.asp?url=/ technet/scriptcenter/monitor/ScrMon22.asp?frame=true.*

2

FS-17: Disk and Volume Management

Activity Frequency: Ad Hoc

Managing file servers also means managing disks, volumes and partitions. The best way to do this is to use the `diskpart` command-line tool. This tool includes its own command interpreter. To launch this command interpreter, open a command prompt and type `diskpart`, then press ENTER. The command interpreter starts and lists a new `diskpart` prompt.

Before you can use this command interpreter, you must `list`, then `select` either a disk, volume or partition to give it focus. The object that has focus will display an asterisk. Use the following command structure within the diskpart command interpreter:

```
list disk (or volume, or partition)
select disk number (or volume label or
partition number)
```

where *number* or *label* are the disk, volume or partition number or, in the case of a volume, its label (such as C, D, E, and so on).

Once an object has focus, you can use the `diskpart` command environment to perform a multitude of management activities on disk objects such as activation, deactivation, extension, creation, deletion, repair, and more.

You can also script `diskpart` activities by creating a simple text-based script file and using the following command:

```
diskpart /s scriptname.txt >logfile.txt
```

By adding *logfile.txt* to the command, you can redirect the script's output to a logfile you can view at a later date.

Diskpart is especially useful if you use WS03's built-in RAID functions.

Print Service Administration

With Windows Server 2003, print service administration involves everything from installing appropriate printer drivers to managing large clusters of print servers supporting massive user communities. In fact, Microsoft has tested a two-server cluster configuration supporting over 3,000 print queues.

WS03 works with Version 3 print drivers—drivers that are designed to integrate more properly with the operating system to provide better fault tolerance. One of the great advantages of these print drivers is that when the printer driver fails, it does not require a server restart but only a print spooler restart. In fact, WS03 can automatically restart the print spooler on a failure making the failure transparent to the majority of the users connected to the printer. The only user who will notice the failure is the one whose job caused the print spooler to fail.

This is because Windows 2000 and 2003 drivers are user-mode drivers as opposed to kernel-mode. Kernel-mode drivers are Version 2 drivers and were used in Windows NT. But a faulty kernel-mode driver can crash the entire kernel—or rather, the entire server. To provide better reliability, Windows 2000 and 2003 drivers were moved to user-mode. In Windows Server 2003, a default Group Policy blocks the use of Version 2 drivers.

TIP *Each printer in WS03 includes a special Troubleshooting topic under the Help menu. This provides you with a series of wizards that help debug printing problems.*

In addition, a default Group Policy blocks remote printer management on new print servers. This policy must be activated before you can manage print servers from the comfort of your desk. You must make sure the Group Policy affecting print servers has the following setting:

- Allow Print Spooler to Accept Client Connections = enabled (**Computer Configuration | Administrative Templates | Printers**)

This will allow you to manage the print server remotely even if no printers are shared on it yet. This policy is automatically activated when you share a printer on a server.

SECURITY SCAN *WS03 supports printer management through a browser, but this requires the installation of Internet Information Server on the print server. In most cases, you should choose not to install IIS on your print servers because IIS can make print server management more complex and WS03 supports several other remote print server management methods.*

SCRIPT CENTER The Microsoft TechNet Script Center includes a series of scripts that help you manage printing in Windows. These scripts can be found at http://www.microsoft.com/technet/treeview/ default.asp?url=/technet/scriptcenter/printing/ default.asp?frame=true. Because of this, script references will not be repeated in each print-related activity unless there is one specific script that addresses the task.

PS-01: Print Queue Management

Activity Frequency: **Daily**

Because printing is a function everyone uses on a daily basis, you should perform a proactive print queue verification on a daily basis. To verify printer status:

1. Launch the **Windows Explorer** (**Quick Launch Area | Windows Explorer**).

2. Navigate to **My Network Places**, locate the print server you need to verify and click **Printers and Faxes**.

3. Click on each printer to view its status. Repair its status if required.

4. In this case, you may have to delete or pause jobs, and then restart the print queue. All of these commands are under the **File** menu.

You can also use the command line to manage print queues:

```
net print \\servername\sharedprintername
```

where *servername**sharedprintername* is the UNC name for the printer. Typing this command lists the details of the print queue. You can also use three switches— /delete, /hold, and /release—to control print jobs. You must provide the job number to do so. For example:

```
net print \\servername\sharedprintername 10 /delete
```

PS-02: Printer Access Management

Activity Frequency: Weekly

SECURITY SCAN *Printer access is controlled through access rights. As always, assigning appropriate and controlled rights is an important aspect of a system administrator's job.*

There are three basic rights that can be assigned to shared printers (**Printer | Properties | Security tab**):

- Print
- Manage Printers
- Manage Documents

These rights control who can do what on a printer. By default, everyone can use a printer once it is shared, but this can be changed. If, for example, you have a brand new color printer that will be reserved for managers only, you need to change its default security settings, removing Everyone and assigning a Managers group the Print right. Anyone with Print rights can manage their own documents on the printer.

By default, Print Operators, Server Operators and Administrators have complete control over shared printers. This means they can manage documents and stop and start printer queues. You must be a member of one of these groups to perform print management activities.

2

PS-03: Printer Driver Management

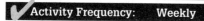
Activity Frequency: Weekly

As mentioned earlier, WS03 uses Version 3 printer drivers. These may not be available for every one of your printers. If this is the case, you will need to monitor printers more closely because Version 2 drivers can halt a server when they fail.

This is the reason why you should regularly monitor the printer manufacturer's web site for new, updated printer drivers for Windows Server 2003. Then, as soon as a Version 3 printer driver is available, modify the shared printer to improve reliability. Make sure the printer driver includes Windows Server 2003 certification. This will guarantee the printer driver's compatibility with WS03.

WS03 includes a default policy that bars Version 2 drivers from being installed (**Disallow installation of printers using kernel-mode drivers** under **Computer Configuration | Administrative Templates | Printers**). If you need to use kernel-mode drivers because you are using older printers, you must disable this policy setting.

TIP *If you deactivate this setting, make it one of your primary objectives to enable it again as soon as possible to improve print server reliability.*

Finally, user-mode printer drivers allow users to set their own printer preferences, but these preferences are derived from the printer properties you set. Make sure you set appropriate properties. For example, if the printer is capable of double-sided printing, set it to print double-sided by default.

PS-04: Printer Sharing

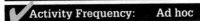

Activity Frequency:	Ad hoc

Printer sharing is the main focus of print server management. Whenever you share printers in Windows Server 2003, you initiate a process that will eventually publish the printer in Active Directory. Users will be able to search the directory for printers based on name, properties, and printer type. Make sure you enter as much detail as possible when preparing a printer for shared use.

To share a printer:

1. Right-click on the printer you want to share and select **Sharing**.

2. Click **Share this printer**, assign a standard **Share name** to the printer and make sure that the **List in the directory** box is checked.

3. If you need to support client systems other than Windows 2000, XP, or 2003, then click **Additional Drivers**.

4. In the Additional Drivers dialog box, check the other Windows systems you need to support, then click **OK**. WS03 will ask you to provide the location of the additional drivers. Identify this location and click **OK**. Click **OK** once again to close the Additional Drivers dialog box.

5. Move to the **Advanced** tab and set spooling properties. Select **Start printing after last page is spooled** and **Print spooled documents first**. Other settings can remain at the default setting.

6. Move to the **Configuration** tab and ensure the device is properly configured. Then move to **Device Settings** and apply default printer settings such as duplex printing, stapling, and paper type in each paper tray.

7. If you need to modify the security settings on the printer share, use **Procedure PS-01**. Click **OK** to close the printer **Properties** dialog box when done.

PS-05: Print Spooler Drive Management

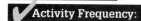

Activity Frequency   Ad hoc

2

Large print servers need to spool a lot of print jobs. This means a lot of disk activity. The best way to provide fast and reliable printing is to dedicate a disk drive (or partition) to print spooling. This means that you need to prepare a special drive and assign the spooling to this drive:

1. In Windows Explorer, open **Printers and Faxes**. Select **Server Properties** from the **File** menu (or use the right mouse button anywhere in the right pane to select **Server Properties** from the context menu).

2. Move to the **Advanced** tab and type in the location for printer spooling. For example, this could be E:\Spool\Printers if E: was your dedicated spooling drive. Click **OK** when done.

Use **Procedure FS-01** on a regular basis to make sure there is enough free space on the print spooler drive.

PS-06: Printer Location Tracking Management

Activity Frequency: Ad hoc

Windows Server 2003 supports Printer Location Tracking. This component is based on the Active Directory site topology designed for your network. One of the key elements of the site topology is the subnet. Each subnet includes a name and a description. It can also include location information. Location information is stored in hierarchical form in the subnet properties under the Location tab. Each level is separated by a slash. You can use up to 256 levels in a location name, though the entire location name cannot be more than 260 characters long. Each part of the name can include up to 32 characters. For example, a printer located in the northeast corner of the first floor of the headquarters building could be identified as HQ/First Floor/Northeast Corner.

To enable Printer Location Tracking in your domain, you need the following elements:

- Subnets and subnet locations entered into Active Directory Sites and Services
- A printer location naming convention
- Location Tracking GPO enabled
- Location settings for all printers
- Location settings for all PCs and servers

To turn Printer Location Tracking on, you must enable the **Pre-populate printer search location** text setting under **Computer Configuration | Administrative Templates | Printers**. This setting enables the Browse button in the Location tab for printer and computer properties within the directory. It also enables this button in the Search Printers tool. Apply this setting in a Group Policy that covers every machine in your network.

Printer location settings are set through the **General** tab of the **Property** dialog box. You can either type or click **Browse** to enter the location. Be as specific as you can.

TIP *You have to perform the same operation on all computer objects in the directory. Open the **Property** dialog box and use the **Location** tab to either type or click **Browse** to enter the location.*

Now, whenever users use the Search tool to locate a printer, printer location will automatically be entered in the location field enabling your user community to find printers near them without having to know your location-naming strategy.

PS-07: Massive Printer Management

Activity Frequency: Ad hoc

WS03 offers a series of Windows Scripting Host scripts to perform local and remote print server management. These include:

- **Prncnfg.vbs** manages printer configurations.
- **Prndrvr.vbs** manages printer drivers.
- **Prnjobs.vbs** manages print jobs.
- **Prnmngr.vbs** manages printers or printer connections.
- **Prnport.vbs** manages TCP/IP printer ports.
- **Prnqctl.vbs** manages print queues.

Each of these commands uses the following command structure:

```
cscript printcommand.vbs
```

where *printcommand* is the name of the script you want to use. Used without switches these commands automatically display help information. These commands are great tools for remote printer management and administration or for scripting operations that affect multiple printers at once.

TIP *You can also perform massive printer modifications with the Microsoft Print Migrator. Search for Print Migrator at http://www.microsoft.com/download for more information.*

PS-08: New Printer Model Evaluation

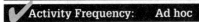
Activity Frequency: **Ad hoc**

Once in a while, you will also need to evaluate new printers. To enforce reliability and simplify your administration overhead, you should make sure all new printers meet the following criteria:

- Printer includes Version 3 digitally signed driver

- Printer driver has "Designed for Windows Server 2003" certification

- Printer is listed on the Microsoft Hardware Compatibility List (HCL) web site (http://www.microsoft.com/hcl/) or includes a certified driver

- Printer includes direct network connectivity

- Printer includes special features

TIP *You may also decide that you do not need to acquire PostScript printers (except in special cases such as for desktop publishing or graphics teams) because the Windows Unidriver rivals PostScript capabilities at lower cost.*

Cluster Services Management

One of Windows Server 2003's main strengths is its capability to support server clusters. WS03 can support server clusters including between two and eight nodes, but it depends on the WS03 edition you use: the Enterprise Edition supports between two and four node clusters and the Datacenter Edition supports between two and eight node clusters. Neither the Web or Standard Editions support server clustering (though they do support Network Load Balancing clusters).

Cluster verification is very important because the very nature of clusters is to provide high availability. This is only possible if it is operating properly. If one node of a two-node cluster is not functioning properly, you no longer have a redundant solution.

There are two cluster administration tools:

- The Cluster Administration console (Start Menu | Administrative Tools | Cluster Administration)
- The `cluster` command-line tool

The latter, the `cluster` command, provides all of the functionality required for cluster administration and can also be scripted. Typing `cluster /?` at the command line provides comprehensive help on this tool.

CS-01: Clusters: Cluster State Verification

Activity Frequency: **Daily**

Cluster services depend upon heartbeat detection to make sure each of the nodes is up and running. If the heartbeat of a node is not detected by the cluster service, it will automatically failover resources to other nodes.

Thus the first thing you should do when verifying the state of your clusters is make sure that each of the nodes is operating properly. Use the following command to do so:

```
ping nodename or nodeipaddress
```

where *nodename* is the node's DNS name or *nodeipaddress* is the physical IP address for the node.

If the nodes do not respond, there may be a problem. Verify the node status with a **Remote Desktop Connection**. You can easily script this procedure and pipe the entire process into a text file (using the `>filename.txt` switch) and simply review the results in your text file.

CS-02: Clusters: Print Queue Status Verification

Activity Frequency: Daily

Server clusters are also very useful as Print Servers because they provide automatic failover on printer failure. But to do so, all printers must use drivers that are updated to meet Windows Server 2003's requirements. Use **Procedure PS-03** to make sure you are using proper print drivers on the server cluster.

Cluster print queues operate the same way as normal print queues except that they provide failover capabilities. To verify the status of the cluster print queues, use **Procedure PS-01**.

CS-03: Clusters: Server Cluster Management

Activity Frequency: Weekly

As mentioned earlier, cluster management is normally performed with either the **Cluster Administrator** console (**Start Menu | Administrative Tools | Cluster Administrator**) or the `cluster` command-line tool. Basically, you must verify that all of the cluster's nodes are operating properly and continue to be configured properly. You use these tools to add or remove nodes, add quorum sets (shared disk storage), and configure majority node set (independent disk storage) replication.

The Cluster Administrator console is the easiest tool to use to add or remove cluster nodes because it includes a comprehensive series of wizards to perform most of the complex clustering tasks. To perform server cluster management:

- Launch the **Cluster Administrator** console. If you haven't already done so, use the **Open Connection to Cluster** dialog box to connect to a server cluster.

- Click on the **Cluster name** and view its status.

- Click on each **Cluster node** and view its status.

- If you have a new application to add to this cluster, right-click on the **Cluster name** and select **Configure Application**.

- This starts the **New Virtual Server** wizard. Provide it with appropriate answers and select the appropriate application type.

Applications can include file shares, print spoolers, DHCP, WINS, Distributed Transaction Coordinator, Message Queuing, Volume Shadow Copies, generic applications, and so on. Each specific application type will change the wizard's behavior and you will be asked appropriate questions for the application type.

You should also verify the System Event Log for events that are generated by the cluster service. These events are from the **ClusSvc** source. Use **Procedure GS-03** to check the System log in the Event Viewer. You can sort events by type simply by clicking on the **Category** column head.

CS-04: Clusters: Quorum State Verification

Activity Frequency: **Weekly**

A quorum is a collection of disks that are shared between cluster members. In WS03, quorums can be of two types: single disk units that are shared between all cluster members or a majority node set. The latter, the majority node set, includes independent disk units for each member of a cluster and can be separated on a geographic basis. The majority node set removes the single point of failure from a server cluster but must rely on replication to operate properly.

The cluster service maintains a Quorum Log and it is through this log that it manages quorum operations. This log file is called **quolog.log** and is located under the **\MSCS** folder of the quorum (%Systemroot%\ Cluster*quorumguid*\MSCS).

TIP   *The Quorum Log is not a regular text file. Do not attempt to modify it.*

Use **Procedure CS-03** to view the quorum's state. Locate the quorum resource under **Clustername | Nodename | Active Resources**, right-click on the quorum name and select **Properties**. This will display the quorum's status under the **General** tab. You can also use the context menu to test failures (**Initiate Failure**) or to take the quorum resource offline (**Take Offline**).

TIP   *Be careful with these operations. Make sure there are no users on the resource before either failure simulations or quorum resource dismounts.*

You can also use the cluster /quorum command to view available quorums. As usual, you can pipe this command to a text file using the >filename.txt switch and you can use this command in a script to automate the procedure.

TIP   *Remember to look in Windows Server 2003's Help and Support Center to find out more information. It includes a special troubleshooting section that is really useful. Just select **Troubleshooting Strategies** from the H&SC home page.*

Chapter 3

Administering Network Infrastructure Servers

A second server role that is critical to the operation of the network is the network infrastructure server. This server includes several different activities, all designed to make sure the underlying network services are functioning properly.

Administrative Activities

The administration of network infrastructure servers is divided into four categories. These include the Dynamic Host Configuration Protocol (DHCP) and/or the Windows Internet Naming Service (WINS) servers, deployment servers such as Remote Installation Services or Automated Deployment Services, network load balancing servers, and servers controlling either remote access or virtual private network connections. Table 3-1 outlines the administrative activities that you must perform on an ongoing basis to ensure proper operation of the networking services you deliver to your user community. It also identifies the frequency of each task.

Note that this table does not include the Domain Naming Service (DNS). Though this service has traditionally been linked to network infrastructures in the past, today it is married to the Active Directory (AD) because it forms the basis of AD's hierarchical structure. As such, it will be covered in Chapter 4.

You may not need to perform all of these activities, because you don't use some of the services mentioned here. For example, large networks rarely rely on Windows Server for remote access. If so, simply ignore the task.

Procedure Number	Activity	Frequency
DHCP/WINS		
DW-01	DHCP Server State Verification	Weekly
DW-02	WINS Server State Vertification	Monthly
DW-03	WINS Record Management	Ad hoc
DW-04	DHCP Attribute Management	Ad hoc
DW-05	DHCP Scope Management	Ad hoc
DW-06	DHCP Reservation Management	Ad hoc
DW-07	DHCP Superscope Management	Ad hoc
DW-08	DHCP Multicast Scope Management	Ad hoc
DW-09	DHCP Option Class Management	Ad hoc
DW-10	DHCP/RIS Server Authorization	Ad hoc
Deployment Servers		
RI-01	RIS Server State Vertification	Monthly
RI-02	RIS Image Management	Ad hoc
NLB Clusters		
NC-01	NLB Cluster State Verification	Weekly
NC-02	NLB Cluster Member Management	Ad hoc
Remote Access/VPNs		
RV-1	Remote Access Server Status Verification	Weekly
RV-02	RADIUS/IAS Server State Verification	Weekly
RV-03	Wireless Monitoring	Weekly
RV-04	Remote Access Policy Verification	Monthly
RV-05	NAT Service Management	Ad hoc
RV-06	VPN Connection Management	Ad hoc

Table 3-1. Network Infrastructure Services Administration Task List

You may also use a different schedule. Remember to personalize the task list to adapt it to your environment.

DHCP/WINS Server Administration

Both the Dynamic Host Configuration Protocol (DHCP) and
the Windows Internet Naming Service (WINS) are services
that have become quite reliable in Windows networks.
This is even more so with Windows Server 2003. This is
one reason why most of the tasks in this category are
performed on an ad hoc basis. In regard to WINS, another
reason is the fact that Windows networks are relying less
and less on this service. Most networks today only include
this service for legacy purposes. You will find that you
will rely less and less on this service as your network
applications evolve. Nevertheless, each verification task
in this list is still performed on at least a monthly basis.

3

The tools most commonly used to manage both DHCP and
WINS are:

- The Global MMC you created in **Procedure GS-17**,
  because it contains access to both services.

- The `netsh` command-line tool that manages both
  DHCP and WINS services. This is a shell command;
  that means, it creates a shell environment when used
  and commands are entered into this shell once the
  focus has been set.

- The `nbtstat` command is also useful with WINS. It
  supports record management from the command line.

DW-01: DHCP Server State Verification

Activity Frequency: **Weekly**

DHCP servers are designed to provide a service that forms
the very basis of a TCP/IP network: addressing. Each time
a new client boots, it contacts the DHCP server to receive
all of the information that will allow it to function on the
network. Therefore, the proper operation of your DHCP
servers is critical.

Once a week, you should verify the proper operation of
your DHCP servers. In most networks, there will be at

least two DHCP servers to provide redundancy for the service. These servers will use the same scopes, but each scope should be divided into 80/20 portions—80 percent being hosted on one server and 20 percent on the other. This allows each DHCP server to provide backup for any given scope. Of course, if you have 50 PCs or fewer, you'll only have a single DHCP server.

To verify the status of your DHCP servers, you need to perform three tasks:

- Check server statistics
- Reconcile scopes
- Check DHCP logs

The first lets you identify how long your server has been running and how well it performs. The second is designed to avoid any errors in IP address leases. DHCP stores both detailed and summary information about a lease. Reconciling scopes allows DHCP to review both sets of information to see if there are any inconsistencies. If inconsistencies are found, they are repaired during this process. The third operation lets you see how your DHCP server behaves on a daily basis (all logs are stored in single-day format).

SECURITY SCAN *You have to be a member of the local DHCP Administrators group or the local Administrators group in order to operate and configure the DHCP server.*

To check server statistics:

1. Launch the **Global MMC Console** (**Quick Launch Area | Global MMC Console**).

2. Connect to the appropriate server (**Action | Connect to another computer**) and either type in the server name (\\servername) or use the **Browse** button to locate it. Click **OK** when done.

3. Move to the **DHCP** service (**Services and Applications | DHCP**).

4. Make sure you click the **DHCP** service and that its information is displayed in the right pane, then right-click on **DHCP** to select **Display Statistics** from the context menu.

5. This will display current statistics for the server, including uptime, discovers, offers, requests, and more. Make note of these values in your weekly DHCP log. Click **Close** when done.

To reconcile scopes:

1. Once again, right-click on **DHCP** and select **Reconcile All Scopes**.

2. Click **Verify** to begin the reconciliation.

3. Click **OK** when DHCP indicates that all scopes are consistent.

4. Click **Cancel** to close the **Reconcile All Scopes** window.

All DHCP events are stored within the System Event Log, but DHCP also writes its own logs. These are stored under %SystemRoot%\System32\DHCP. These logs are enabled by default (see Figure 3-1).

To view DHCP logs:

1. Use the **Global MMC Console** to open a **Remote Desktop Connection** to the DHCP server (**Computer Management** I Remote Desktops I *connectionname*).

2. When the connection is open, launch **Windows Explorer** (**Quick Launch Area** I **Explorer**).

3. Move to the **%SystemRoot%\System32\DHCP** folder.

4. Double-click on any of the last week's logs to view them. Log files are named DHCPSrvLog-*day*.log where *day* is the three character abbreviation for the day of the week. Each of the seven log files are written over every week.

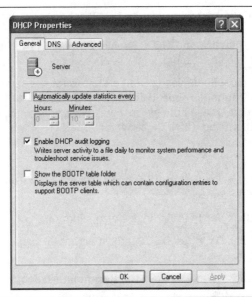

Figure 3-1. DHCP audit logging is enabled by default. This setting can be found in the DHCP server's properties.

> **TIP** *The amount of space available on the server for logging purposes will determine the amount of information DHCP will store in these log files. Make sure sufficient space is available. By default, the minimum log size is 20MB and the maximum is 70MB.*

The DHCP server also stores logging information in the System Event Log, but the information stored in its own log files is much more complete.

You can also use command-line tools to view information about the server. This means using the `netsh` command within the DHCP scope. To view server information interactively, use the following commands:

```
netsh
dhcp
server servername
show all
```

where *servername* is the DNS name of the server you want to connect to. Basically, the first command opens the `netsh` console, the second sets the DHCP scope, the third sets focus on a specific server, and the last requests information about the server. To exit the `netsh` console, type:

```
quit
```

3

TIP *To view information about* `netsh dhcp` *commands, type* `/?` *at the* `netsh dhcp>` *command prompt.*

To automatically collect information about a DHCP server, type:

```
netsh dhcp server servername show all >filename.txt
```

where *servername* is the DNS name of the DHCP server and *filename.txt* is the name of the output file you want the information stored in. You can put a series of these commands in a command file and use **Procedure GS-19** to automatically generate the output files every week. This helps you quickly identify the state of all DHCP servers in your network.

TIP *Note the structure of the* `netsh` *command. It works interactively if you press* ENTER *after you type each portion of a command, or it works in batch mode if you type an entire command string at once.*

DW-02: WINS Server State Verification

 Activity Frequency: **Monthly**

Even though WINS servers are only used to support legacy applications, they are still required in most large networks. Once a month, you should verify the proper operation of your WINS servers. In most networks, there will be at least two WINS servers to provide redundancy for the service. These servers should be replication partners using persistent connections.

To verify the status of your WINS servers, you need to perform three tasks:

- Check server statistics.
- Scavenge the database to remove stale records.
- Check WINS logs for errors.

You may also check database consistency and check for version ID consistency. The latter deals with how WINS manages replication. Each record is given a version ID. The records with the highest version ID are replicated to the server's partners.

 *You have to be a member of the local WINS Users group or the local Administrators group in order to operate and configure the WINS server.*

To check server statistics:

1. Launch the **Global MMC Console** (**Quick Launch Area | Global MMC Console**).

2. Connect to the appropriate server (**Action | Connect to another computer**) and either type in the server name (\\servername) or use the **Browse** button to locate it. Click **OK** when done.

3. Move to the **WINS** service (**Services and Applications | WINS**).

4. Make sure you click the **WINS** service and that its information is displayed in the right pane, then right-click on **WINS** to select **Display Server Statistics** from the context menu.

5. This will display current statistics for the server, including uptime, discovers, offers, requests, and more. Make note of these values in your monthly WINS log. Click **Close** when done.

You can use the same context menu to select Scavenge Database, Check Database Consistency, and Check Version ID Consistency.

You can also use command-line tools to view information about the server. This means using the `netsh` command within the WINS scope. To automatically collect information about a WINS server, type:

```
netsh wins server servername show statistics
>filename.txt
```

where *servername* is the DNS name of the WINS server and *filename.txt* is the name of the output file you want the information stored in. You can put a series of these commands in a command file and use **Procedure GS-19** to automatically generate the output files. You can also include the `init scavenge` command in these files to automatically initiate scavenging on your servers.

TIP *You can also collect information interactively by typing each command alone. To view information about* netsh WINS *commands, type* /? *at the* netsh wins> *command prompt.*

WINS servers in Windows Server 2003 support dynamic database compaction. This means that each time the server database has been updated and the server is idle, it will try to recover lost space within its database. Unfortunately, this does not recover all lost space. Therefore, you should manually compact the database at least once a month to recover all lost space. To do so, you must take the WINS server offline.

Use the following series of commands to stop the service, compact the database, and restart the service:

```
sc \\servername stop wins
timeout /t 300
netsh wins server servername init compact
sc \\servername start wins
```

Here, the `timeout` command is required to make sure the WINS service has been stopped before the compaction begins. You can insert these commands in a command file and use **Procedure GS-19** to automatically perform this operation on a monthly basis.

DW-03: WINS Record Management

Activity Frequency: Ad hoc

Once in a while, the WINS record of a given machine does not appear in the database. This may be so for a variety of reasons: the client cannot find the WINS server, the server is busy when a record arrives and cannot include it in its database, the server did not replicate a record, and so on.

This is where the nbtstat command becomes useful. It can be used to refresh NetBIOS information on individual computers. The simplest command for this is:

```
nbtstat -RR
```

This command releases information held in the WINS server and refreshes NetBIOS information locally. It must be performed on the machine whose record is to be updated.

For more information on this command, type nbtstat at the command prompt.

DW-04: DHCP Attribute Management

Activity Frequency: Ad hoc

Along with IP addresses, DHCP servers provide IP address attributes to their clients. These attributes are either global (that is, they are provided to all clients) or local (that is, they are provided to only those clients within a given address scope). These attributes may change from time to time, so you will need to modify existing attributes or add new attributes.

In the DHCP console, these attributes are called *scope options*. Global scope options should include at least the following:

- 003 Router: The address of a router.
- 006 DNS Servers: The address of at least two DNS servers.

- 015 DNS Domain Name: The domain name for the scope.

- 044 WINS/NBNS Servers: The address of at least two WINS servers.

- 046 WINS/NBT Node Type: This should be set to H-node. H-node resolution is best even in wide area networks because it greatly reduces the amount of broadcasting on each network.

3

TIP *DNS servers are set globally here to ensure all clients always have a valid DNS address; however, in Windows Server 2003, with the coming of Active Directory, the DNS service is married to the Domain Controller service, placing a DNS server wherever there is a DC. Thus, you need to override these global values by local scope values, because local scope options should now include the local DNS server since DNS is now integrated to Active Directory. In addition, each client must find the closest DNS server, which is usually one that is local to its network (especially in regional offices).*

To configure scope options:

1. Launch the **Global MMC Console (Quick Launch Area | Global MMC Console**).

2. Connect to the appropriate server (**Action | Connect to another computer**) and either type in the server name (\\servername) or use the **Browse** button to locate it. Click **OK** when done.

3. Move to the **DHCP** service (**Services and Applications | DHCP**).

4. To modify global options, right-click on **Server Options** and choose **Configure Options** from the context menu.

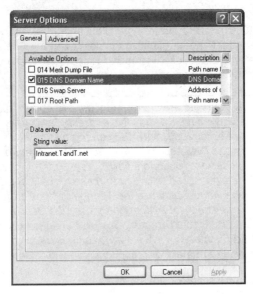

5. Configure or modify the options you require (or as outlined earlier). Click **OK** when done.

This will set the global options for all scopes on this server.

To configure local scope options, expand the scope by clicking on it and use the same procedure, but this time with **Scope Options**.

To modify either global or local scope options through the command line, use the following command:

```
netsh dhcp server servername add optiondef parameters
```

where *servername* is the DNS name of the DHCP server and *parameters* includes the details of the modification you want to make. Use `add optiondef /?` for the details of the parameters setting.

DW-05: DHCP Scope Management

Activity Frequency: **Ad hoc**

Once in a while, you will also need to add, remove, or modify DHCP scopes. If you use the 80/20 rule for scope redundancy (creating a scope on two servers and enabling 80 percent of the scope on one and 20 percent on the other), you will need to create each scope and exclude the appropriate range on each server. Once all scopes are created, you must join them into a superscope. Superscopes are scope groupings that allow the DHCP server to service more than one subnet. They are required whenever multinetting is used. Use the superscope to include all of the scopes in a set of server ranges. The content of superscopes should be the same on each of the servers you manage. Use **Procedure DW-07** for superscope management.

3

TIP *It is also very important to fully document your DHCP information. An excellent DHCP address worksheet is available from the TechRepublic web site at http:// www.techrepublic.com/download_item.jhtml?id=r002200 20409van01.htm&src=search. You must be a member to access this worksheet.*

To configure a DHCP scope:

1. Launch the **Global MMC Console** (**Quick Launch Area | Global MMC Console**).

2. Connect to the appropriate server (**Action | Connect to another computer**) and either type in the server name (\\servername) or use the **Browse** button to locate it. Click **OK** when done.

3. Right-click on the **DHCP** item and select **New Scope** from the context menu. DHCP will launch the **New Scope Wizard**. This wizard allows you to input all of the values for the scope: **starting address, end address, exclusions**, and even **scope-specific options**.

4. You can choose to **Activate** the scope or not at the end. It is best to skip activation at this stage. This

lets you review all of your settings before the scope
begins to service requests.

5. Remember to exclude **80 or 20 percent** of the scope,
depending on where you want the main portion of
the scope to be hosted.

To modify scopes, right-click on the scope and select
Properties. To delete a scope, **deactivate** it first and then
delete it through the context menu.

To create or delete a scope through the command line, use
the following commands:

```
netsh dhcp server servername add scope parameters
netsh dhcp server servername delete scope parameters
```

where *servername* is the DNS name of the DHCP server
and *parameters* includes the details of the modification
you want to make. Use `add scope /?` or `delete scope /?`
for the details of the parameters setting.

DW-06: DHCP Reservation Management

Activity Frequency: **Ad hoc**

Address reservations are used to ensure that specific
machines always receive the same address but still profit
from dynamic addressing. Examples of where you would
use address reservations are servers, domain controllers,
and client machines that run applications that may have
hard-coded IP addresses.

To make sure each machine always receives the same
address, you should configure your address reservations
on each DHCP server that can respond to requests from
machines requiring a reservation. This ensures that these
clients don't receive a dynamic address by mistake.

TIP *You will need the MAC address for each of the
network cards for which you want to reserve an IP address.
MAC addresses can be displayed by typing* `ipconfig`
`/all` *at the command prompt of the system for which the
reservation is required.*

To configure an address reservation:

1. Launch the **Global MMC Console** (**Quick Launch Area | Global MMC Console**).

2. Connect to the appropriate server (**Action | Connect to another computer**) and either type in the server name (\\servername) or use the **Browse** button to locate it. Click **OK** when done.

3. Select the appropriate scope to create reservations within it. Click **Reservations** in the left pane, then right-click on **Reservations**.

4. Choose **New Reservation** from the context menu.

5. Fill in the **reservation details**. Close the dialog box by clicking **Add**. Repeat as necessary.

TIP *If you use DHCP to assign static addresses to servers, you should make sure that the Alternate Configuration for Internet Protocol (TCP/IP) Properties for each network card are set to the same values as the reservation. Use* ***Control Panel | Network Connection*** *to view the IP Properties for each network card.*

DW-07: DHCP Superscope Management

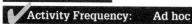 **Activity Frequency:** **Ad hoc**

Superscopes are groupings of scopes that support the assignment of multiple scopes managing different subnets from the same server. Superscopes regroup all of these scopes into a single management group. One advantage of using superscopes is that you can activate the entire superscope and all its scopes in one fell swoop.

TIP *Superscopes cannot be created until at least one scope has been created on a DHCP server.*

To create a superscope:

1. Launch the **Global MMC Console** (**Quick Launch Area | Global MMC Console**).

2. Connect to the appropriate server (**Action |
   Connect to another computer**) and either type in
   the server name (\\servername) or use the **Browse**
   button to locate it. Click **OK** when done.

3. Once at least one scope has been created, right-click
   on **DHCP** and select **New Superscope.** This will launch
   the **New Superscope Wizard**. Click **Next** to proceed.

4. Name the Superscope, then select **the scopes** that
   will be part of this superscope. Close the dialog box
   when done.

Once a superscope is created, new scopes can be added
to it in one of two ways: the scope can be created within
the superscope by right-clicking on the **Superscope Name**
and selecting **New Scope,** or the scope can be created
outside the superscope and added to the superscope once
created. This is done by right-clicking on the **scope** and
selecting **Add to Superscope.**

Scopes all need activation before they can begin to service
clients. You can activate multiple scopes at once by
activating a superscope. Review each scope's settings
to make sure they are appropriate, then activate the
superscope. To do so, right-click on the **superscope name**
and select **Activate** from the context menu.

TIP *Scope activation can also act as a failsafe mechanism
because you can create spare scopes on each server before
they are actually required and activate them only when
they are required.*

DW-08: DHCP Multicast Scope Management

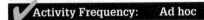

Activity Frequency: **Ad hoc**

Multicasting is different from unicasting in that a single
address is used by multiple clients. The advantage of a
multicast is that a single broadcast can be received by
multiple clients at once, significantly reducing network
traffic. Multicasting can be used when sending large files
to several clients and in order to reduce overall network

traffic. Examples of multicast use are videoconferencing, large software deployments, and audio streaming.

The Windows Server 2003 DHCP server can also support the allocation of multicast scopes. When it does so, it operates using the Multicast Address Dynamic Client Allocation Protocol (MADCAP). Multicast address ranges are concentrated on Class D IP addresses. These range from 224.0.0.0 to 239.255.255.255. Addresses in this class can only be used for multicasting.

When using multicast scopes internally, you tend to work with administrative multicast scopes. The range most recommended for this scope begins with 239.192.0.0 and uses a subnet mask of 255.252.0.0 (14 bits in length). This range is known as the *IPv4 Organization Local Scope* and is intended for use by organizations setting multicast scopes privately for internal use. Using this address, you can create up to 262,144 group addresses.

To create a multicast scope:

1. Launch the **Global MMC Console** (**Quick Launch Area | Global MMC Console**).

2. Connect to the appropriate server (**Action | Connect to another computer**) and either type in the server name (\\servername) or use the **Browse** button to locate it. Click **OK** when done.

3. Right-click on the **DHCP** item and select **New Multicast Scope** from the context menu. DHCP will launch the **New Multicast Scope Wizard**. This wizard allows you to input all of the values for the scope: **scope name, description, starting address, end address**, and **exclusions**.

4. You can also **Activate** the scope through the wizard. However, do so only if you are sure all your settings are correct.

5. Click **Finish** when done.

You can also create multicast scopes through the command line. Use the following command:

```
netsh dhcp server servername add mscope parameters
```

where *servername* is the DNS name of the DHCP server and *parameters* includes the details of the modification you want to make. Use `add mscope /?` for the details of the parameters setting.

DW-09: DHCP Option Class Management

✔ **Activity Frequency:** Ad hoc

Windows Server 2003 supports the use of classes within DHCP. Two classes are supported: user and vendor classes. Each can be used to identify specific machines and provide these with particular settings. One example of a useful user class is a special user class for mobile clients. By identifying mobile clients, you can differentiate them from desktop clients and set their lease duration to a shorter time period than those of the PC workstations in your network. Thus, when a mobile user goes from one site to another, addresses are released when they leave the site.

User classes are quite useful when you want to designate special DHCP assignments to specific classes of machines in your network. Vendor classes are usually used when you can guarantee that users all have machines originating from the same vendor. Both classes make it possible to address client subsets through DHCP. Both must be used together to function properly.

To define user classes:

1. Launch the **Global MMC Console** (**Quick Launch Area | Global MMC Console**).

2. Connect to the appropriate server (**Action | Connect to another computer**) and either type in the server name (\\servername) or use the **Browse** button to locate it. Click **OK** when done.

3. Right-click on **DHCP** and select **Define User Classes.**

4. Click **Add** in the **User Class** dialog box.

5. In the **New Class** dialog box, type the class **Display Name** and **Description**, and then *place your cursor*

directly below the word ASCII. *Type in the* **Class Name**. You will note that the **New Class** dialog box inputs the binary values for each ASCII character as you type them. *Do not modify these values!* Also, class names are case sensitive. You'll need to make note of how you spelled the class name. Click **OK** when done.

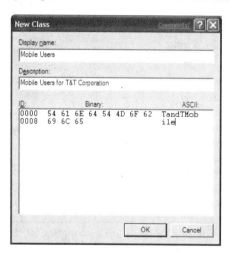

6. Repeat the process for each class you need to add. When all classes have been added, click **Close** to return to the Global MMC console.

7. Next, right-click on the **Server Options** item and select **Configure Options.** Move to the **Advanced** tab and select **Microsoft Windows 2000 Options** as the vendor class and **Mobile Users** as the user class.

8. Set the value for **number 02, Microsoft Release DHCP Lease on Shutdown Operating System** by clicking on the **check box**.

9. Next change the vendor class to **DHCP Standard Options** to set **option 51, Lease**. The value is in the 0x*seconds*, where seconds is the number of seconds for lease duration. For example, 0x86400 means 24 hours.

10. Finally, you will need to set this user class on all mobile systems. To do so, you need to use the `ipconfig` command on each computer. This setting can be performed at PC staging. The command structure is as follows:

```
ipconfig /setclassid adapter_name
class_id
```

For example, if your class ID is "TandTMobile," the command would be

```
ipconfig /setclassid Local Area Connection
TandTMobile
```

TIP *Class IDs are case sensitive. You must type in the exact class ID wording for it to work properly.*

User-defined class options can be assigned to either server or scope options, depending on whether they apply to systems in all scopes or only to systems in specific scopes.

TIP *User-defined classes are also useful for the assignation of domain names to systems that are located in the same physical locations but use multiple domains. For example, if you have users in the same physical location that use different domains, such as an intranet and a development domain, you can use a user-defined class to make sure that systems register DNS values in the proper DNS domain controller. Use the user-defined class only for the smallest number of systems. This will make it easier to stage and manage the systems.*

To add a class through the command line, use the following commands:

```
netsh dhcp server servername add class parameters
```

where *servername* is the DNS name of the DHCP server and *parameters* includes the details of the modification you want to make. Use `add class /?` for the details of the parameters setting.

DW-10: DHCP/RIS Server Authorization

In a Windows Server 2003 network using Active Directory, servers that will affect multiple systems must be authorized. This includes DHCP services as well as Remote Installation Services (RIS). This feature is designed to make sure that rogue machines cannot send out false addresses to clients. It is also quite useful because you can configure your server, review all settings, and correct potential errors before putting the server into service.

SECURITY SCAN *Server authorization can only be done by users with the proper credentials. You must be a Domain Administrator to activate a server.*

To authorize a server:

1. Launch the **Global MMC Console** (**Quick Launch Area | Global MMC Console**).

2. Connect to the appropriate server (**Action | Connect to another computer**) and either type in the server name (\\servername) or use the **Browse** button to locate it. Click **OK** when done.

3. Depending on the service you are authorizing, right-click on **DHCP** and select **Manage authorized servers** from the context menu.

4. Click **Authorize**, type the name of the server to authorize, and click **OK**.

5. Click **Close** when done.

Your server is now ready to service clients.

TIP *It may be necessary to use the DHCP console to perform this task (**Manage Your Server | Manage this DHCP server**) because sometimes the **Manage authorized servers** command does not appear in the Global MMC or Computer Management Console.*

Deployment Servers

Windows Server 2003 includes several deployment technologies. The most useful of these are Remote Installation Services (RIS) and Automated Deployment Services (ADS). RIS can be used for both servers and workstations. ADS can only be used for servers. Both of these technologies are more powerful than other deployment services because they support both the initial staging and the reconstruction of a machine. Both are also activated through the use of a Preboot Execution Environment (PXE) network card. This means that you can start a new machine that does not include an operating system—press F12 during the boot sequence, boot from the network interface card, and select the operating system to install from the menu choices that are presented to you.

The major difference between RIS and ADS lies with the image that is downloaded to the machine. RIS uses a modified version of an unattended installation to deploy the OS to a machine. It saves time because it does not need to send all installation files to the machine it is staging—it only sends those files that will actually be used during setup. ADS uses a combination of disk imaging and remote installation to stage servers. Because it uses a disk image, it is faster and less complicated to use than RIS.

Another difference is in the way both services supply machines with IP addresses. Since RIS uses the boot sequence of a network card to contact the machine to be staged, it must supply this machine with an IP address, in much the way DHCP does. Because of this, RIS must also be authorized in Active Directory to function.

This is not the case for ADS since it relies on an existing
DHCP server to supply addresses to machines as they
boot from the network card.

Both servers are mostly managed through the graphical
interface (since you normally have only few of these types
of servers in any network).

*TIP ADS is an add-on to Windows Server 2003 and
should be released before the end of 2003. For more
information on ADS, go to http://www.microsoft.com/
technet/treeview/default.asp?url=/technet/prodtechnol/
windowsserver2003/evaluate/technologies/deploy/
VCON67.asp.*

RI-01: RIS Server State Verification

Activity Frequency: Monthly

A RIS server includes a series of complex technologies
working together. For this reason, it is important to verify
its state on a regular basis. This task is set to a monthly
frequency, which should be appropriate for most networks,
but if your RIS servers are supporting large client bases
that must be staged or reconstructed on a regular basis, you
may want to increase the frequency of this task to weekly.

To verify a RIS server:

1. Launch the **Global MMC Console** (**Quick Launch
   Area | Global MMC Console**).

2. Move to **Active Directory Users and Computers**.

3. Locate the RIS server you want to verify (**Forest |
   Domain | Organizational Unit | RIS Server**) and
   right-click on it to select **Properties**.

4. Move to the **Remote Installation** tab and click **Verify Server**.

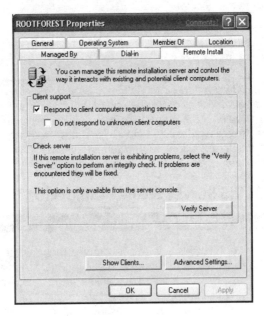

5. This launches the **Verify Server Wizard**. Follow the prompts and click **Finish** when done.

This operation can also be used to restore a RIS server to a working state.

RI-02: RIS Image Management

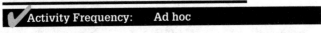

Activity Frequency: **Ad hoc**

Every now and then, you will need to either modify or update RIS installation images. Modification comes when new components are added to completed images such as service packs, hot fixes, and other program updates.

RIS supports two types of images: generic and custom. A generic image is based on the content of the Windows Server Installation CD. It is created simply by using RIS to copy the installation files to the server. A custom image is generated from a preinstalled or reference server that has been customized to meet your requirements. During image capture, RIS depersonalizes this installation and copies it to the server. Custom RIS image captures are nondestructive; that is, the server can still be used after the image has been captured.

You need to use the Remote Installation Preparation Wizard (RIPrep.exe) to create a custom image:

1. Install and customize the **Reference Server**. This should include any additional software as well as the customization of elements such as the default user profile, desktop personalization, and tool settings.

2. Use **Windows Explorer** (**Quick Launch Area | Windows Explorer**) to navigate to the RIS server's shared distribution folder.

3. Locate the **Admin\I386** folder and open it. This folder contains all of the client preparation tools.

4. Locate and launch **RIPrep.exe**. This launches the Remote Installation Preparation Wizard. This wizard helps you make the required choices for the preparation of your image. Click **Next**.

5. Name the **image**, click **Next**, and select a **shared folder** to store it in. Click **Next**.

6. Add a **Friendly description** and **Help text** (information to help identify what is in the image). Click **Next**.

7. Next, RIPrep will stop all extraneous services. This makes it easier to copy service state information. Only bare networking services are required to connect to the RIS server and copy the disk image. Click **Next**.

8. Review the settings summary and click **Next**.

9. Click **Next** to begin the imaging process. The wizard will:
   - Verify the Windows version.
   - Analyze disk partitions.

- Copy partition information to the server.
- Copy system files to the server.
- Copy and update Registry information.
- Shut down the system.
10. Your image is now ready. When you restart the system, it will reset the information (such as the Security Identifier) modified by the RIPrep process.

You will also need to edit and customize the Unattended setup file used for installation. This file is located within the I386 folder of your image on the RIS server. It ends in .SIF for "setup information file." The default RIS Unattended answer file is named RISTNDRD.SIF. Now you're ready to deploy the image you have created.

NLB Clusters

The Network Load Balancing (NLB) service provides high availability and scalability for IP services (both TCP and UDP) and applications by combining up to 32 servers into a single cluster. Clients access the NLB cluster by accessing a single IP address for the entire group. NLB services automatically redirect the client to a working server. NLB services are installed by default on Windows Server 2003. NLB clusters are very useful for load balancing terminal services, streaming media, Web applications, and virtual private network servers.

Two tools are used to manage NLB clusters:

- The NLB Manager is a graphical interface that provides access to all of the NLB management commands. NLB Manager is the preferred management tool.

- `nlb.exe` is a command-line tool that is designed to manage NLB clusters. Remote control must be enabled on the cluster for `nlb.exe` to work.

SECURITY SCAN *It is highly recommended that you avoid activating remote control on NLB clusters and avoid using the* `nlb.exe` *command-line tool, because it exposes the cluster to potential damage from people with malicious intent. Use NLB Manager instead.*

You can also start the NLB Manager from the command line using `nlbmgr.exe`.

NC-01: NLB Cluster State Verification

Activity Frequency: Weekly

NLB clusters are composed of several servers responding to like requests. One of the best ways to identify the status of the NLB cluster is to enable logging and to verify the logging file on a regular basis.

To enable logging:

1. Launch the **NLB Manager** (**Start | Administrative Tools | NLB Manager**).

2. Select **Log Settings** from the **Options** menu.

3. In the **Log Settings** dialog box, check **Enable Logging** and type in the name of the log file. Locate the file in **C:\Toolkit** and name it **NLBLog.txt**.

4. Click **OK** to close the dialog box.

From now on, all NLB activity will be logged in the NLBLog file. This file is quite useful even though all activity is displayed in the bottom pane of the NLB Manager window, because the NLB Manager only displays information about the current session while the log file provides information about all sessions.

To review the status of the NLB cluster, locate the NLBLog file and double-click on it. Review the information stored in the file. Review this file on a weekly basis.

NC-02: NLB Cluster Member Management

Activity Frequency: Ad hoc

Once in a while, you will need to enable and disable NLB cluster members for maintenance and other purposes. Use the NLB Manager to do so:

1. Use the **Global MMC** to connect to a member of the NLB cluster (**Remote Desktop | Connection Name**).

2. Launch the **NLB Manager** (**Start | Administrative Tools | NLB Manager**).

3. Select **Connect to Existing** from the **Cluster** menu.

4. In the **Connect** dialog box, type in the name of a host, press **Connect**, then select the cluster name and click **Finish**.

5. To add a host to the cluster, right-click on the cluster name and select **Add Host to Cluster**. Follow the instructions in the wizard to complete the operation.

6. To stop a host for maintenance purposes, right-click on the host name and select **Control Host | Stop**. Use the same procedure with **Control Host | Start** to restart the host once maintenance has been performed on the host.

7. Close the **NLB Manager** when done.

Managing your NLB hosts should be relatively straightforward.

Remote Access/VPNs

The Routing and Remote Access Service (RRAS) in Windows Server 2003 has changed significantly since Windows NT. It now supports several functions:

- Remote access management and authorization

- Virtual private network (VPN) connections

- Wireless access management

- Routing within networks

- Connection sharing or Network Address Translation (NAT)

While few organizations of any size use all of the features of the RRAS service, many use both the Remote Access Service (RAS) and VPN connections, especially if they use wireless networks.

Several tools are available for managing these services. Once again, the Global MMC Console created in **Procedure GS-17** will be useful for management through the graphical interface. For those who prefer to use the command line, the `netsh` command will provide most of the functionality they require.

RV-01: Remote Access Server Status Verification

Activity Frequency: **Weekly**

The first administrative activity linked to RAS is the verification of the status of your remote access servers. This should be done on a weekly basis.

To verify the status of a RAS server:

1. Launch the **Global MMC Console** (**Quick Launch Area | Global MMC Console**).

2. Connect to the appropriate server (**Action | Connect to another computer**) and either type in the server name (\\servername) or use the **Browse** button to locate it. Click **OK** when done.

3. Move to **Routing and Remote Access** (**Computer Management | Services and Applications | Routing and Remote Access**) and click it once.

4. Click **Server Status**. The status of the server, including the number of connections it currently manages, will be displayed in the right window pane.

5. Make note of the server status in your weekly report.

You should also review the RAS server activity log. This log is stored in the %SystemRoot%\System32\LogFiles folder by default. To review the log:

1. Use the **Global MMC** to connect to the RAS server you want to verify (**Remote Desktop | Connection Name**).

2. Launch **Windows Explorer** (**Quick Launch Area | Windows Explorer**) and move to the **%SystemRoot%\System32\LogFiles** folder.

3. Locate the current week's log file and double-click on it. The log file name is **INyymmww.log**.

4. Make note of any anomalies in the file.

TIP   *Before you can view RAS log files, you must configure them. Configuration is performed under **Remote Access Logging (General MMC I Services and Applications I Routing and Remote Access I Remote Access Logging**). Double-click on **Local File** to set logging parameters. Select each of the items you want to log on the **Settings** tab and set the log file format as well as the new file frequency on the **Log File** tab. Make sure the new file frequency is set to **Weekly**.*

RV-02: RADIUS/IAS Server State Verification

Activity Frequency: Weekly

With Windows Server 2003, RAS authentication can be performed through the Internet Authentication Service (IAS). This service simplifies authentication for RAS users. The most important administrative activity linked to IAS is the verification of the status of your authentication servers. This should be done on a weekly basis.

To verify the status of an IAS server:

1. Launch the **Global MMC Console** (**Quick Launch Area I Global MMC Console**).

2. Connect to the appropriate server (**Action I Connect to another computer**) and either type in the server name (\\servername) or use the **Browse** button to locate it. Click **OK** when done.

3. Move to **Internet Authentication Service** (**Computer Management I Services and Applications I Internet Authentication Service**) and click it once.

4. Click **RADIUS Clients**. This will display current connection requests.

5. Make note of any anomalies in your weekly report.

You should also review the IAS server activity log. This log is stored in the %SystemRoot%\System32\LogFiles folder by default and uses the same settings as the RAS logs created in **Procedure RV-01**.

RV-03: Wireless Monitoring

✔ **Activity Frequency:** Weekly

Wireless network administration is focused on two facets: client connections and access point status. Both can be found in the Wireless Monitor snap-in. This snap-in was included in the General MMC Console created in **Procedure GS-17**.

To monitor wireless activity:

1. Launch the **Global MMC Console** (**Quick Launch Area | Global MMC Console**).

2. Connect to the appropriate server (**Action | Connect to another computer**) and either type in the server name (\\servername) or use the **Browse** button to locate it. Click **OK** when done.

3. Move to **Wireless Monitor** (**Computer Management | Wireless Monitor**) and click it once.

4. To view the status of the access points in your network, click **Access Point Information**.

5. To view the status of wireless clients in your network, click **Wireless Client Information**.

You can also log all wireless client activity. To do so, you must turn on wireless client logging by right-clicking on **Wireless Client Information** (**Wireless Monitor | *servername* | Wireless Client Information**) and selecting **Enable Logging**. Log files are stored under the %SystemRoot%\System32\LogFiles folder.

RV-04: Remote Access Policy Verification

✔ **Activity Frequency:** **Monthly**

3

Unlike Windows NT, Windows Server 2003 manages remote access through policies. These policies are an ordered set of rules that define whether access is granted or denied. Each policy consists of a set of conditions, a profile set to which the conditions are applied, and a set of remote access permissions. Policies are applied in the order they are listed.

The best way to manage remote access policies is by integrating RAS to the RADIUS service through IAS. This allows you to centrally manage all RAS policies. Another advantage is that all access policies can be managed in one single location. This includes policies for virtual private network connections, wireless connections, and remote access.

Because RAS policies are managed through IAS, the best way to verify the status of your policies is to use **Procedure RV-02**. Policy settings are located under **Computer Management | Services and Applications | Internet Authentication Service | Remote Access Policies**.

RV-05: NAT Service Management

✔ **Activity Frequency:** **Ad hoc**

The Windows Server Routing and Remote Access Service also includes the ability to support Network Address Translation (NAT). In fact, the Windows Server NAT service also includes a rudimentary firewall. The NAT service is quite useful in regional or branch office scenarios where multiple systems are routed through a single external connection. NAT also supports virtual private networking, making it a useful tool for interconnecting remote offices.

To manage the NAT service:

1. Launch the **Global MMC Console** (**Quick Launch Area | Global MMC Console**).

2. Connect to the appropriate server (**Action | Connect to another computer**) and either type in the server name (\\servername) or use the **Browse** button to locate it. Click **OK** when done.

3. Move to **NAT/Basic Firewall** (**Computer Management | Services and Applications | Routing and Remote Access Service | IP Routing | NAT/Basic Firewall**) and click it once.

4. To review the status of this service, right-click on it and select **Show DHCP Allocator Information**, then right-click on it again and select **Show DNS Proxy Information**. Both windows display the information currently allocated by the NAT service.

5. Close both windows when done.

TIP   *If your network is using Active Directory, as it should, you will not use the NAT service to allocate DNS information, but only to allocate DHCP addresses. DNS information is closely tied to the Active Directory service and must be implemented separately from the NAT service.*

RV-06: VPN Connection Management

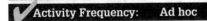

Activity Frequency: Ad hoc

Finally, virtual private network connections are also managed through Routing and Remote Access. These include external connections from clients accessing the internal network as well as VPN tunnels between servers such as in the connection of branch offices to larger sites.

VPN connections running on Windows Server 2003 can use either the Point to Point Tunneling Protocol (PPTP) or the Layer 2 Tunneling Protocol (L2TP). You should aim to use the latter wherever possible. It works in conjunction with the IPSec protocol to provide more secure connections than PPTP.

To create a new VPN interface:

1. Launch the **Global MMC Console** (**Quick Launch Area | Global MMC Console**).

2. Connect to the appropriate server (**Action | Connect to another computer**) and either type in the server name (\\servername) or use the **Browse** button to locate it. Click **OK** when done.

3. Move to **Network Interface**s (**Computer Management | Services and Applications | Routing and Remote Access | Network Interfaces**) and click it once.

4. Right-click **Network Interfaces** and select **New Demand-Dial Interface** from the context menu. This launches the **Demand-Dial Interface Wizard**. Click **Next**.

5. Name the interface and click **Next**.

6. Select **Connect using virtual private network** and click **Next**.

7. Select **Automatic selection** or, if you are certain you want to use L2TP, select **L2TP** and click **Next**.

8. Enter the name of the destination address in host name format and click **Next**.

9. Select **Route IP packets on this interface** and **Add a user account so a remote router can dial in** and click **Next**.

10. Add the static route for this interface. Use the **Add** button to add each part of the route, then click **Next**.

11. Type in the password for the dial-in connection, click **Next**, then type the credentials for the dial-out connection and click **Next**.

12. Click **Finish** to create the interface.

From now on, right-click on the interface and select **Properties** to review its settings.

Chapter 4

Administering Identity Servers

Active Directory is the very core of the Windows Server network. It manages user identity and computer accounts; controls groups; supports object structuring and organization through forests, domains, and organizational units; and, through the power of Group Policy, it controls the behavior of the objects it contains.

Administrative Activities

The administration of identity servers is divided into two categories. These include the management of domain controllers and all the objects they contain as well as the administration of the Domain Naming System (DNS) servers. DNS servers are included here because this service is at the very basis of Active Directory. Without a fully functional DNS service, Active Directory would be completely unreachable since all of its own services are based on the DNS hierarchical structure and DNS records. In fact, to ensure proper AD operation, each domain controller should also host the DNS service. This is the reason why the DNS service is not located in Chapter 3 in this book.

Table 4-1 outlines the administrative activities that you must perform on an ongoing basis to ensure proper operation of the services you deliver to your user community. It also identifies the frequency of each task.

You may not need to perform all of these activities, because you may not use some of the services mentioned here. You may also use a different schedule. Remember to personalize the task list to adapt it to your environment.

Procedure Number	Activity	Frequency
Domain Controllers		
DC-01	User Management	Daily
DC-02	User Password Reset	Daily
DC-03	Directory Service Log Event Verification	Daily
DC-04	Account Management	Daily
DC-05	Security Group Management	Daily
DC-06	KCC Service Status Management	Weekly
DC-07	AD Replication Topology Verification	Weekly
DC-08	Global Catalog Status Verification	Weekly
DC-09	Universal Administration Group Management	Weekly
DC-10	Account Policy Verification	Weekly
DC-11	PKI Service Verification	Weekly
DC-12	AD Service/Admin Account Verification	Monthly
DC-13	Lost and Found Object Management	Monthly
DC-14	Right Delegation Management	Ad hoc
DC-15	Software Installation Management	Ad hoc
DC-16	GPO Management	Ad hoc
DC-17	Computer Object Management	Ad hoc
DC-18	Distribution Group Management	Ad hoc
DC-19	AD Forest Management	Ad hoc
DC-20	AD Information Management	Ad hoc
DC-21	Schema Management	Ad hoc
DC-22	Schema Access Management	Ad hoc
DC-23	Schema Content Modification	Ad hoc
DC-24	Schema-Modifying Software Evaluation	Ad hoc
DC-25	Operations Master Role Management	Ad hoc

Table 4-1. Identity Server Administration Task List

Procedure Number	Activity	Frequency
DC-26	Operations Master Role Transfer	Ad hoc
DC-27	Operations Master Disaster Recovery	Ad hoc
DC-28	Domain Controller Promotion	Ad hoc
DC-29	Domain Controller Disaster Recovery	Ad hoc
DC-30	Trust Management	Ad hoc
DC-31	Forest/Domain/OU Structure Management	Ad hoc
DC-32	Active Directory Script Management	Ad hoc
DC-33	Forest Time Service Management	Ad hoc
DC-34	Access Control List Management	Ad hoc
DC-35	Managing Saved Queries	Ad hoc
DC-36	Managing Space within AD	Ad hoc
DC-37	Managing the LDAP Query Policy	Ad hoc
DC-38	Managing the AD Database	Ad hoc
Namespace Management (DNS)		
DN-01	DNS Event Log Verification	Daily
DN-02	DNS Configuration Management	Monthly
DN-03	DNS Record Management	Ad hoc
DN-04	DNS Application Partition Management	Ad hoc

Table 4-1. Identity Server Administration Task List (*continued*)

Domain Controller Administration

Domain controller administration is really Active Directory administration. Though you will need to manage the operation of the domain controllers themselves, you also need to manage the content of the Active Directory. This means using a wide variety of tools, both in graphical and command-line mode. The tools you use to manage AD include:

- The three AD consoles: Users and Computers, Sites and Services, and Domains and Trusts.

- The Group Policy Management Console (GPMC), a single-purpose console that must be downloaded from the Microsoft web site (search for GPMC at http://www.microsoft.com/download).

- The `csvde` command-line tool, which is designed to perform massive user and computer account operations.

- The `ds` commands (for Directory Service), a series of commands supporting the administration of directory objects.

- The `ldifde` command, a powerful tool that even lets you modify AD schemas or database structures.

- The `ntdsutil` command, which is specifically designed to manage the AD database.

- A series of commands oriented towards Group Policy administration such as `gpresult`, which identifies the result of Group Policy Object (GPO) application; `gpupdate`, which updates GPOs on a system; and the `dcgpofix` tool, which resets GPOs to their default setting (at installation).

Since the AD service is so critical to the proper operation of a Windows Server 2003 network, several activities are performed more frequently than with other services.

__SCRIPT CENTER__ The Microsoft TechNet Script Center includes a series of Windows Scripting Host (WSH) sample scripts that help you perform user and group administration tasks. These scripts can be found at http://www.microsoft.com/technet/treeview/ default.asp?url=/technet/scriptcenter/user/ default.asp?frame=true. Because of this, script references will not be repeated in each user- or group-related activity unless there is one specific script that addresses the task.

DC-01: User Management

✓Activity Frequency: Daily

User management is set to a daily frequency because in larger networks, user account creation or modification is required on a regular basis. This activity is mostly initiated by request forms that come from your user base. As such, it is often performed on an ad hoc basis during the day because many administrators perform it when the request comes in. But, if you want to structure your day so that you perform activities in an organized manner, you should collect all user account creation/modification requests and perform this activity only in a set period of each day.

To create a new user object:

1. Launch the **Global MMC Console** (**Quick Launch Area | Global MMC Console**). The console automatically connects to your default domain. If you need to work with a different forest or domain controller, right-click on **Active Directory Users and Computers** (**Computer Management | Active Directory Users and Computers**) and select the appropriate command to change your connection.

2. Navigate to the appropriate organizational unit (OU). If you are using the default Windows structure, this should be the Users container (**Computer Management | Active Directory Users and Computers | *domainname* | Users**).

TIP   The default Users container in AD is not an organizational unit and therefore cannot support either delegation or the assignation of Group Policy objects. GPOs must be assigned at the domain level to affect this container. If you want to assign GPOs to user objects but not at the domain level, you must create a new People OU.

---

3. Either right-click in the right window pane to select the **New | User** command in the context menu or use the **New User** icon in the console toolbar. This activates the **New Object - User Wizard**.

4. This wizard displays two dialog boxes. The first deals with the account names. Here you set the user's full name, the user's display name, their logon name or their user principal name (UPN), and their down-level (or Pre-Windows 2000) logon name. Click **Next**.

5. The second screen deals with the password and account restrictions. Type in the password for this user and make sure the checkbox for **User must change password at next logon** is selected. If the user is not ready to take immediate possession of the account, you should check the **Account is disabled** option as well. Click **Finish** when done.

SECURITY SCAN   *Be careful when you set a password to never expire. If it is for a nonuser account such as a service account—accounts that are designed to operate services—or for a generic purpose account, you should also make sure you set the **User cannot change password** option. This way, no one can use the account to change its password.*

You can also use much the same procedure to modify existing accounts and perform operations such as disabling accounts, renaming them, and reassigning them.

TIP   *Windows Server 2003 supports two types of logon names: the UPN and the down-level logon name. The latter is related to the Windows NT logon name you used to give to your users. If you are migrating from a Windows NT environment, make sure you use the same down-level name strategy (unless there are compelling reasons to change this strategy). Users will be familiar with this strategy and will be able to continue using the logon name they are most familiar with. Down-level logon names work mostly within a single domain whereas UPNs are mostly used to cross domain boundaries.*

You can also automate the user creation process. The csvde command is designed to perform massive user modifications in AD. Use the following command to create multiple users at once:

```
csvde -i -f filename.csv -v -k >outputfilename.txt
```

where $-i$ turns on the import mode, $-f$ indicates the source file for the import (*filename.csv*)—this source file must be in comma-separated value (CSV) format, $-v$ puts the command in verbose mode, and $-k$ tells it to ignore errors and continue to the end. You can review the *outputfilename.txt* file for the results of the operation.

TIP   *CSV files can easily be created in Microsoft Excel. They usually contain a first line indicating which values are to come. For example:* CN,Firstname,Surname,Description *should support values such as:* jdoe,Jane,Doe,Manager *or* japscott,John,Apscott,Technician *and so on. Once created, use Excel to save the file as a* **CSV (Comma Delimited)** *file.*

If you need to migrate information from one domain to another, use the csvde command to first export the information, then import the information from one domain to the other. Type csvde -? for more information.

TIP   *You can also create two other types of user objects.* **InetOrgPerson** *is a user object that has exactly the same properties as a User object. It is used to maintain compatibility with other, non-Microsoft directory services.* **Contact** *is a user object that cannot be a security principal. It is created only to include its information in the directory.*

DC-02: User Password Reset

Activity Frequency: Daily

The most common activity administrators must perform on user accounts is the password reset. This is the reason why this is set as a daily task. Depending on the size of your network, you may not have to reset passwords daily, but chances are good you have to do it more than once a week.

TIP   *In order to avoid replication latency, especially when you reset a password for a regional user, you should always connect to the user's closest domain controller to reset the password. This way, users don't have to wait for the change to be replicated from central DCs to regional DCs to be able to use the new password.*

To reset a user's password:

1. Begin by launching the **Active Directory Users and Computers** portion of the Global MMC and right-click on it to select **Connect to Domain Controller**. Select the proper DC and click **OK**.

2. Once connected, right-click on the domain name and select **Find**.

3. Type the user's name in the **Find** dialog box and click **Find Now**.

4. Once you locate the proper user, right-click on their name and select **Reset Password**.

5. In the **Reset Password** dialog box, type the new password, confirm it, and check **User must change password at next logon**. Click **OK** when done.

6. Notify the user of the new password.

You can also change passwords through the command line:

```
dsmod user "UserDN" –pwd a5B4c#D2eI –mustchpwd yes
```

where the *UserDN* is the user's distinguished name. For example, "CN=Jane Doe, CN=Users, DC=Intranet, DC=TandT, DC=Net" refers to user Jane Doe in the Users container in the Intranet.TandT.Net domain. Use quotes to encompass the entire username.

The directory also stores a lot of information that is not necessarily available to users. One example is user account information. A new tool, acctinfo.dll can be found in the Account Lockout Tools (search for it at www.microsoft.com/download). This tool must be registered on the server or workstation using the Active Directory Users and Computers console:

```
regsvr32 acctinfo.dll
```

Once registered, it adds a new tab to the user object's Property page, the Additional Account Info tab. This tab is quite useful because it provides additional information

about the status of the account and also provides a button
for resetting regional user passwords directly on their site
DC, avoiding replication delays.

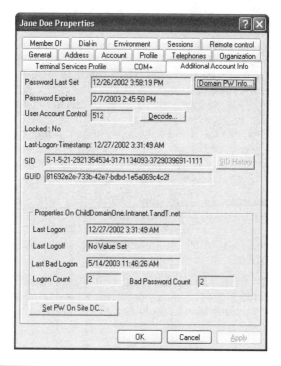

TIP   *If you want to use this DLL in the Global MMC, you
will need to reopen the console in author mode, remove
the AD Users and Computers snap-in and add it anew.
Review **Procedure GS-17** to see how to perform this
operation.*

SCRIPT CENTER   *The Microsoft TechNet Script
Center includes a script that supports changing user
passwords. This script can be found at http://
www.microsoft.com/technet/treeview/default.asp?url=/
technet/scriptcenter/user/ScrUG03.asp?frame=true.*

DC-03: Directory Service Log Event Verification

✔ Activity Frequency: Daily

The Active Directory Service stores all of its information in a special Event Log, the Directory Services log. Like all logs, this log is located under the Event Log heading in the Computer Management portion of the Global MMC Console. This log lists events related to directory operation. It covers the Knowledge Consistency Checker (KCC) service whose job is to verify and update the replication topology of your DCs; it covers directory replication; it covers the status of the AD database, NTDS.DIT (located in the %SystemRoot%\NTDS folder); and much more.

Use **Procedure GS-03** to view the Directory Services log, but through the Global MMC instead of the Computer Management console. You can export the data for reference, or you can make note of any anomalies and proceed to repair them.

Like all other logs, the DS log includes significant information about repairing problems when they occur. Log this activity in your Daily Activity Log (**Procedure GS-06**).

DC-04: Account Management

✔ Activity Frequency: Daily

User account management activities can range from a simple modification of the data contained in the user account to massive account creation. This is why several tools are associated with these activities.

Also, since there are more than 200 attributes associated with the user account, most organizations share the data management burden among different roles. Users, for example, are responsible for updating their own information in the directory. This includes their address, their role in the organization, and other location-specific information. User representatives are often responsible for workgroup-related information in the directory: who the user works for, in which department, and so on. Administrators are then left with user account creation, password resets, account lockout termination, and other service-related tasks. Users update their own information via the Windows Search tool; they search for their name in the directory, then modify the fields that are available to them. User representatives usually work with delegation consoles and have access to only those objects they are responsible for in the directory. Administrators use the Active Directory Users and Computers console.

4

Computers also have manageable accounts in Active Directory. They are also contained in a special container in the directory by default: the Computers container. Like the Users container, the Computers container is not an OU.

TIP *Microsoft offers an add-on that lets you right-click on a computer account and select Remote Control. This add-on is called the Remote Control Add-on for Active Directory Users and Computers. Search for it at www.microsoft.com/downloads.*

Use **Procedures DC-01** and **DC-02** to either create new accounts or modify existing ones.

TIP *You can also use the* `csvde` *command outlined in* **Procedure DC-01** *to preload the directory with computer names. This is really helpful when you need to install new machines and you want to create all of the computer accounts in a specific OU.*

DC-05: Security Group Management

✔ Activity Frequency: Daily

Windows Server 2003 supports two types of groups:

- Security groups that are considered security objects and that can be used to assign access rights and permissions. These groups can also be used as an email address. Emails sent to the group are received by each individual user that is a member of the group.

- Distribution groups that are not security enabled. They are mostly used in conjunction with email applications such as Microsoft Exchange or software distribution applications such as Microsoft Systems Management Server 2003.

SECURITY SCAN *Groups within native Windows Server forests can be converted from one type to another at any time. Therefore, if you find that a group no longer requires its security features, you can change it to a Distribution group and remove its access rights.*

In addition to group type, Windows Server supports several different group scopes. Group scopes are determined by group location. If the group is located on a local computer, its scope will be local. This means that its members and the permissions you assign to it will affect only the computer on which the group is located. If the group is contained within a domain in a forest, it will have either a domain or a forest scope. The domain and forest modes have an impact on group functionality. In a native Windows Server forest, you are able to work with the following group scopes:

- Domain Local Members can include accounts (user and computer), other domain local groups, global groups, and universal groups.

- Global Members can include accounts and other global groups from within the same domain.

- Universal Members can include accounts, global groups, and universal groups from anywhere in the forest or even across forests if a trust exists.

Groups, especially security groups, have specific functions. These functions are based on the UGLP Rule. This rule is outlined in Figure 4-1. As you can see, users should be placed in Global Groups, Global Groups are placed in Domain Local Groups, and permissions are assigned to the Domain Local Groups. Universal Groups are used to bridge domains and forests by placing Global Groups within them and placing them within Domain Local Groups to grant access to resources.

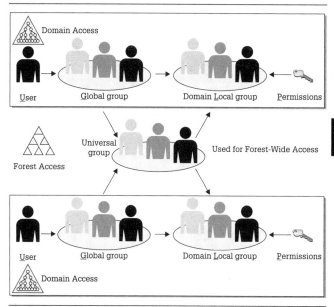

Figure 4-1. The UGLP Rule

The UGLP Rule makes it simple to determine which group type you need to create because it contains logic. This logic is displayed in Figure 4-2.

Use Figure 4-2 to determine both group scope and group type when creating groups. This will greatly simplify group management.

Use **Procedure DC-01** to create groups. Choose **New | Group** from the context menu. Follow both the process in Figure 4-2 and the wizard's instructions to create the group. If you are sure of what you want to create, use the following command:

```
dsadd group "groupDN" -secgrp yes -scope scope
-desc description
```

where *groupDN* is the group's distinguished name and *scope* is either "l", "g", or "u" for each of the available scopes. *Description* is the description you want to add to the group.

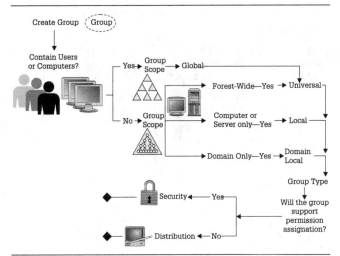

Figure 4-2. The group creation process flow chart

To manage the users in a group, first use **Procedure DC-02** to locate the group, then double-click on the group name. Move to the **Members** tab, then click **Add**. Type in the names of the objects to add and click **Check Names**. If several results are displayed, select the appropriate object(s) and click **OK**. Click **OK** to add the object. Click **OK** to close the **Group Properties** dialog box.

TIP   *You can also navigate to the container in which the objects you want to add are stored, select them, right-click on them, and select **Add to Group** to add multiple objects at once.*

DC-06: KCC Service Status Management

✓ Activity Frequency: Weekly

Replication is at the core of Active Directory. Replication occurs within a given site if there is more than one DC in the site and between sites if there are DCs located in different sites. By default, intersite replication routes are managed by the Knowledge Consistency Checker (KCC) service. For this to occur between sites, at least one site link must be created between each site that contains a domain controller. This site link includes costing information. It will also include replication scheduling information; that is, when the DC is allowed to replicate.

The KCC uses the site link, site link schedule, and costing information to determine when to replicate, how to replicate (which route to take), and the number of servers to replicate with. Data that is replicated between sites is also compressed. AD compresses replication data through a compression algorithm. Data is automatically compressed whenever it reaches a certain threshold. Usually, anything greater than 50 KB will automatically be compressed when replicated between sites.

SECURITY SCAN *Special values such as password changes or account deactivations are replicated immediately to the PDC Emulator in the domain despite site-specific schedules. This ensures that lockouts and password changes are immediately available to the entire domain.*

To verify the frequency of your intersite replication:

1. Begin by launching the **Active Directory Sites and Services** portion of the Global MMC.

2. Navigate to the **IP Inter-site Transport (Computer Management | Active Directory Sites and Services | Sites | Inter-site Transports | IP)**.

3. Right-click on the **Site Link** you want to verify and select **Properties**.

4. The replication frequency is in the **General** tab under **Replicate Every**.

5. Click **OK** when done.

You can also use **Procedure DC-03** to check for KCC-related messages in the Directory Services Event Log. To perform a KCC consistency check, use the `repadmin` command:

```
repadmin /kcc DC_List
```

where *DC_List* is the list of the DCs you want to check. You can also use the /asynch switch to avoid starting a replication immediately if you have multiple DCs in your list.

TIP *The* repadmin *command is also very useful to display information about different aspects of replication. Use* repadmin /? *for more information.*

SCRIPT CENTER *The Microsoft TechNet Script Center includes a series of Windows Scripting Host (WSH) sample scripts that help you perform service administration tasks. These scripts can be found at http://www.microsoft.com/technet/treeview/default.asp?url=/technet/scriptcenter/services/default.asp?frame=true.*

DC-07: AD Replication Topology Verification

Activity Frequency: **Weekly**

This procedure is closely related to **Procedure DC-06**. For the KCC to work properly, the site topology must be properly defined. It is a good idea to verify the status of your site topology once a week at the same time as you perform the KCC Service Verification. Once again, this relies on the verification of the Directory Services Event Log for replication-oriented errors. Use **Procedure DC-03** to do so.

There are several important factors that make intersite replication work. One of the most important is the replication latency of your network. Replication latency is calculated by multiplying the number of replication hops between the furthest ends of your wide area network by the replication frequency you have set. For example, if you have three hops (Site 1 must send it to Site 2, Site 2 to Site 3, and Site 3 to Site 4) and your replication frequency is the default 180 minutes, it will take 3 times 180 minutes or 540 minutes to replicate a change that was made in Site 1 to Site 4. Keep this in mind when you design your replication topology.

To verify the replication topology:

1. Begin by launching the **Active Directory Sites and Services** portion of the Global MMC.

2. Navigate to the **NTDS Settings (Computer Management | Active Directory Sites and Services | Sites | *sitename* | Servers | *servername* | NTDS Settings**) where *sitename* and *servername* are the site and server you want to verify, and click it.

3. Right-click on **NTDS Settings** to select **Check Replication Topology (All Tasks | Check Replication Topology**).

4. Click **OK** to close the **Check Replication Topology** dialog box.

5. Press the F5 key or select the **Refresh** icon in the toolbar to refresh the connections in the right pane.

You can also use the same procedure to force replication if you need to:

1. Select **NTDS Setting**s and move to the right pane and select the link you want to verify.

2. Right-click on the link to select **Replicate Now** from the context menu.

3. Click **OK** to close the **Replication Status** dialog box.

There are also two command-line tools that can be used to verify replication status. To verify the replication status on a specific DC:

```
repadmin /showreps servername
```

where *servername* is the DNS name of the server you want to check. To validate DNS connections for replication:

```
dcdiag /test:replications
```

This command will list any replication errors between domain controllers. You can pipe the results of both commands to a filename to save the information. Enter any anomalies in your weekly activity log.

SCRIPT CENTER The Microsoft TechNet Script Center includes two sample scripts that help you perform AD replication administration. The first enumerates the replication partners in AD and the second monitors AD replication. These scripts can be found at http://www.microsoft.com/technet/treeview/ default.asp?url=/technet/scriptcenter/monitor/ default.asp?frame=true. It also includes several scripts for site management. These can be found at http:// www.microsoft.com/technet/treeview/default.asp?url=/ technet/scriptcenter/network/default.asp?frame=true.

DC-08: Global Catalog Status Verification

Activity Frequency: **Weekly**

The Global Catalog is crucial to the proper operation of an Active Directory. Without it, no one can find any of the objects stored in the directory. So, its proper operation must be verified on a regular basis.

Global Catalogs contain two types of information: objects that have been marked as globally useful and therefore must be available everywhere and at all times, and universal group memberships. It is for this reason that at least one domain controller in each site should be designated as a Global Catalog server (GCS). In addition, each site should be set to Cache Universal Group Memberships. This should greatly reduce the amount of replication required between Global Catalog Servers.

TIP As outlined in **Procedure DC-05**, universal groups should only contain other groups, principally global groups. This way, they do not need to replicate information when global group membership is modified because as far as the universal group is concerned there has been no change.

To verify that Global Catalog information is available in remote sites:

```
dsquery * -gc -s servername
```

where *servername* is the name of the remote server you want to verify. The -gc switch also makes sure it is a Global Catalog Server that answers the request. This command should return a list of 100 results (the default volume of the output from the dsquery command). If this query does not work, use **Procedure DC-07** to force replication.

You can also automate this process by placing it in a command file along with **Procedure GS-19**.

To make a DC a GCS:

1. Begin by launching the **Active Directory Sites and Services** portion of the Global MMC.

2. Navigate to the **NTDS Settings (Computer Management ∣ Active Directory Sites and Services ∣ Sites ∣ *sitename* ∣ Servers ∣ *servername* ∣ NTDS Settings**) where *sitename* and *servername* are the site and server you want to modify, and click it.

3. Right-click on **NTDS Settings** and select **Properties** from the context menu.

4. Check the **Global Catalog** option on the General tab. Click **OK** to close the **Properties** dialog box.

To set Universal Group Membership Caching:

1. Begin by launching the **Active Directory Sites and Services** portion of the Global MMC.

2. Navigate to the site you want to modify (**Computer Management ∣ Active Directory Sites and Services ∣ Sites ∣ *sitename***) where *sitename* is the site you want to modify, and click it.

3. Move to the right pane and right-click on **NTDS Site Settings** to select **Properties** from the context menu.

4. Check **Enable Universal Group Membership Caching** and click **OK** to close the dialog box.

SCRIPT CENTER *The Microsoft TechNet Script Center includes three sample scripts that help you perform Global Catalog server administration. The first two enable or disable the Global Catalog function on a DC and the third locates GC servers. These scripts can be found at http://www.microsoft.com/technet/treeview/ default.asp?url=/technet/scriptcenter/compmgmt/ default.asp?frame=true.*

DC-09: Universal Administration Group Management

Activity Frequency: **Weekly**

Windows Server 2003 includes two Universal Administration Groups: Enterprise Administrators and Schema Administrators. These groups are granted the highest rights in an AD forest. By default, you should make sure the Schema Administrators group is empty. It should contain a user only when an actual schema modification is required (see **Procedure DC-22**). The Enterprise Administrators group should also be tightly controlled. This is why this operation is a weekly activity.

Windows Server includes a group policy that will automatically restrict the number of users in these groups. This policy is located at:

- **Computer Configuration | Windows Settings | Security Settings | Restricted Groups**

You should add both universal administration groups to this policy. The Schema Administrators group should be set to be empty by default. The Enterprise Administrators group should only contain authorized administrative accounts. Use **Procedure DC-16** to modify this policy.

SECURITY SCAN *To make sure this policy is applied to all, make this setting in the Default Domain Policy of the root domain of each of the forests you manage.*

Even though you set this policy, it is possible for someone with enough administrative rights and the proper skills to circumvent it for brief time periods (GPOs are refreshed every five minutes on DCs). This is why you should regularly check the membership of these groups to make sure no one has modified them and added themselves into the groups.

SECURITY SCAN *It is a good idea to create the same type of Restricted Group policy for the Domain Administrators group in each of the domains in your forest because this group also has elevated rights.*

4

DC-10: Account Policy Verification

Activity Frequency: Weekly

The Account Policy is the policy that determines how accounts are managed within a given domain. This policy is usually stored within the Default Domain Policy in order to ensure that it affects all objects in the domain. The Account Policy is located under **Computer Configuration | Windows Settings | Security Settings**. Recommended settings for this policy are listed in Table 4-2. Adapt them to your own requirements.

You need to verify this policy regularly to make sure that no one has modified it inadvertently. Use **Procedure DC-16** to verify that your Account Policy has not been modified.

SECURITY SCAN *Strong passwords are enabled by default in Windows Server 2003. For more information on what constitutes a strong or complex password, search for "strong passwords" in the Help and Support Center.*

TIP   All of the recommended settings for the Kerberos Policy are set at the Windows Server default, but setting them explicitly assists your Group Policy operators in knowing what the default setting actually is.

Setting	Recommendation	Comments
Account Policy ǀ Password Policy		
Enforce password history	24 passwords	At the rate of one password change per month, this setting remembers two years' worth of passwords.
Maximum password age	42 days	This is approximately a month and a half.
Minimum password age	2 days	This stops users from changing their passwords too often.
Minimum password length	8 characters	This is the threshold where password crackers start taking longer to break passwords.
Password must meet complexity requirements	Enabled	This ensures that passwords must contain both alphabetic and numeric characters, both uppercase and lowercase, as well as special symbols.
Store passwords using reversible encryption	Disabled	Enabling this setting is the same as storing plaintext passwords. This setting should never be enabled.
Account Policy ǀ Account Lockout Policy		
Account lockout duration	60 minutes	This setting determines how long an account is locked after several bad logon attempts.
Account lockout threshold	3 invalid logon attempts	After three bad logon tries, the account is locked out.
Reset account lockout counter after	60 minutes	This must be equal to or greater than the account lockout duration.
Account Policies ǀ Kerberos Policy		
Enforce user logon restrictions	Enabled (default)	This ensures that users have the right to access either local or network resources before being granted a Kerberos ticket.

Table 4-2. Recommended Account Policy Settings

Setting	Recommendation	Comments
Maximum lifetime for service ticket	600 minutes (default)	This states the duration of the session ticket that is used to initiate a connection with a server. It must be renewed when it expires.
Maximum lifetime for user ticket	10 hours (default)	This must be greater than or equal to the previous setting. It must be renewed when it expires.
Maximum lifetime for user ticket renewal	7 days (default)	This details the duration of a user's ticket-granting ticket. The user must log on again once this ticket expires.
Maximum tolerance for computer clock synchronization	5 minutes (default)	Kerberos uses time stamps to grant tickets. All computers within a domain are synchronized through the domain controllers.

Table 4-2. Recommended Account Policy Settings
(continued)

DC-11: PKI Service Verification

Activity Frequency: **Weekly**

Certificate services are used in a variety of instances within a Windows Server network. They support the Encryption File System; they also support wireless authentication; they support virtual private network connections; and, when used with Software Restriction Policies, they can certify your scripts and software packages—protecting you from scripted viruses. Managing the Public Key Infrastructure (PKI) service in Windows Server can be done either through the Certificate Authority snap-in or through the `certutil` command.

Use the following command to view the status of a certificate server:

```
certutil –cainfo –config camachinename\caname
```

where *camachinename* and *caname* are the computer name and Certificate Authority name for the targeted machine.

The `certutil` command is very powerful and supports almost every operation related to certificate management in Windows Server 2003. For more information on this command, type `certutil /?` at the command prompt.

TIP *You can also use the Certificate Manager to view the certificates associated with computer or user accounts. To do so, locate the CertMgr.msc console (in %SystemRoot%\ System32) and double-click on it. You can also launch this tool by searching for Certificate in the Windows Server Help and Support Center.*

DC-12: AD Service/Admin Account Verification

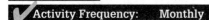

Activity Frequency: Monthly

Procedure GS-05 outlines how to create both service and administrative accounts. It also outlines how to modify their password on a regular basis. Both administrative and service accounts are privileged account types because they have both access rights and rights assignments that other account types do not. This is why you should take the time to verify the status of these accounts on a monthly basis. This will help you ensure that there are no abuses or errors in either the use of these accounts or the way they are configured.

Use **Procedure DC-16** to verify the status of rights assignments set for service accounts. Use **Procedure DC-09** to make sure the group membership of all privileged accounts is tightly controlled. Enter the information in your activity log.

DC-13: Lost And Found Object Management

Activity Frequency: Monthly

Once in a while, especially in large forests, someone will delete a container at the same time someone else is creating an object in this container. This can be on entirely different DCs, but when replication occurs to synchronize data on the DCs, the newly created object no longer has a home. When this happens, Active Directory automatically stores objects within the LostAndFound container. This special container manages lost and found objects within the domain. Another special container, the LostAndFoundConfig container, manages lost and found objects for the forest. The latter is in the forest root domain only.

Therefore, once a month you should verify the LostAndFound and the LostAndFoundConfig containers for objects to determine if these objects should be moved to new containers or simply deleted from the directory.

To verify the LostAndFound containers:

1. Begin by launching the **Active Directory Users and Computers** portion of the Global MMC.

2. Make sure the advanced view is activated (**View | Advanced Features**) and click the **LostAndFound** container.

3. Identify any objects located within this folder. Decide if they need to be moved to other containers or if you should delete the objects.

TIP *Be careful when deleting objects. Make sure you review the object's properties before doing so. Sometimes, it is best to move the object and deactivate it while you communicate with your peers to see if it is a necessary object. Remember, once deleted, SIDs are gone forever.*

DC-14: Right Delegation Management

Activity Frequency: Ad hoc

Active Directory management in complex environments relies on the concept of delegation. In AD, it is easy to delegate management activities. Delegations can be performed at several levels: sites, organizational units, or even entire domains.

TIP *Delegation is mostly done with organizational units. Sites and domains should rarely be delegated.*

Delegation is performed through the Delegation of Control Wizard. In addition to the delegation of control, you often have to create custom consoles to give delegated administrators access to the objects you have delegated to them. If the console is based on a particular snap-in, you will also have to make sure it is installed on the user's computer before they can use the custom console.

SECURITY SCAN *You can also perform some degree of delegation through the use of Windows Server's built-in groups. Windows Server includes special groups for Account, Backup, Network Configuration, Group Policy, DNS, Print, and Server administration as well as Performance Monitoring, Certificate Publishing, and Help Services management. These groups should be used in conjunction with the AD Delegation Wizard to delegate operations in AD.*

To delegate rights in Active Directory:

1. Begin by launching the **Active Directory Users and Computers** portion of the Global MMC.

2. Locate the object you want to delegate and right-click on it to select **Delegate Control** from the context menu. This launches the Delegation of Control Wizard. Click **Next**.

3. Click the **Add** button to select the groups you want to delegate to. Type the name of the group and click

Check Names. Select the proper group from the results and click **OK**. Click **Next**.

4. Select the tasks you want to delegate and click **Next**. Alternatively, you can create a custom task to delegate; this will change the behavior of the wizard and ask you which specific task you want to delegate on which object type.

5. Click **Finish** to close the wizard and complete the delegation.

To create a custom console, you need to start the console program in authoring mode in the same way as **Procedure GS-17**:

1. Open a command console and run the following **command** (the /a parameter is only required if you are not logged in as an administrator):

```
mmc /a
```

2. This launches an empty MMC. Move to the **File** menu and select **Add/Remove Snap-in**. In the **Snap-in** dialog box, click the **Add** button. Select the snap-in or snap-ins you require—for example, Active Directory Users and Computers. **Close** the **Add Snap-in** dialog box when done.

3. Many snap-ins include extensions. To view extensions, use the **Extensions** tab. Deselect all of the extensions that are not required. For example, if you are delegating user management in AD, you do not need any of the Active Directory Users and Computers extensions. Click **OK** when done.

4. Save your console (**File | Save**) and give it an appropriate name. Select the OU you want to delegate, right-click on it, and select **New Window from Here** from the context menu. Close the former window so that only the new window is open.

5. Next, create a Taskpad view for the console. Right-click on the OU and choose **New Taskpad View** from the context menu. This launches the Taskpad Wizard. Click **Next**.

6. Select the list format for the console and the style for task descriptions. Click **Next** when done.

7. Set the task view for **All tree items that are the same type as this tree item** and click **Next**.

8. Name the Taskpad view and give it a description. Click **Next**.

9. Make sure the **Start New Task Wizard** option is checked and click **Finish** to complete the Taskpad.

10. The **New Task Wizard** will launch. Click **Next**. Select **Menu Commands** and click **Next**. You can also add navigation tasks or scripted commands. To add navigation tasks, you must have added the appropriate OUs to your Favorites first.

11. Select **List in the details pane** and click the menu task required for the delegation, then click **Next**.

12. Add the appropriate icon and click **Next**. Click **Finish** to complete the task creation. If you need to add another task, check **Run this Wizard again**. **Save** the console again.

13. Set the view options for this window. You can remove a number of items, such as the console tree, standard menu, standard toolbar, and so on. Move to the **View** menu and select **Customize**. Deselect all of the **items** you do not deem necessary for console users. Click **OK** when done.

TIP *This dialog box is live; when you deselect an item, you immediately see the result in the console behind the dialog box.*

14. Finally, you need to customize the console. Move to the **File** menu and select **Options**. Here you can type in a **console description**, assign a **new icon** (the Shell32.dll file contains several icons that can be used to customize MMCs), and determine the **console operation mode**. There are four console operation modes:

- **Author mode**   Gives you complete control of the MMC.

- **User mode, full access**   The same as author mode, but users cannot add snap-ins, change options, and create Favorites or Taskpads.

- **User mode, limited access, multiple windows**   Gives access only to the selected items when the console was saved. Users can create new windows, but cannot close any previously saved windows.

- **User mode, limited access, single window**   Same as preceding, but users cannot create new windows.

15. For single-purpose consoles, select **User mode, limited access, single window**. Click **OK** when done. **Save** and close the console.

Test the console to ensure it operates as designed. Open it in operation mode (as opposed to authoring mode) by double-clicking on its icon.

TIP   *There are a lot of different options to use for Taskpad creation. Take the time to try them out to view the results. This will help you identify those that suit your environment best.*

You can distribute the console to a group by sending them the console file, but if the console is based on a snap-in they do not have installed, you will need to install the snap-in first. This can be done through Group Policy using software distribution. If you choose to use Group Policy for snap-in installation, you can include the console as well in the same Windows Installer executable (see **Procedure DC-15**).

DC-15: Software Installation Management

Group Policy can be used for a wide variety of management activities, one of which is the remote delivery of software to either users or machines. It is preferable to target machines when delivering software, because users can move from system to system and thus receive an installation several times.

Software can be assigned or published through GPOs. Assigned software is automatically installed on targeted machines. Published software will appear in the Add/Remove Programs item of the Control Panel. Users can then choose to install it or not. Published software should only include products that are deemed optional in your network. All other software should be assigned.

In addition, all software must be packaged in Windows Installer format. This can be done with a variety of tools, the best of which are Wise for Windows Installer (www.wise.com) or Package Studio (also from Wise Solutions Inc.), or Installshield Admin Studio (www.installshield.com). This is one area where you don't want to try to work with free tools because they are quite cumbersome.

To assign a software package:

1. Begin by placing the Windows Installer setup file (msi extension) in a shared folder.

2. Launch the **Group Policy Management Console** portion of the Global MMC.

3. Navigate to the **Group Policy Objects** container (**Computer Management** I **Group Policy Management** I **Forest:** *forestname* I **Domains** I *domainname* I **Group Policy Objects**).

4. Locate the GPO to edit or create a new GPO to edit (right-click in the right pane and select **New**, name

it, and click **OK**). Since software is assigned to computers, right-click on the GPO and select **User Settings Disabled** from the **GPO Status** menu item.

5. Right-click on the GPO to edit and select **Edit**. This launches the GPO Editor.

6. Navigate to **Software Installation** (**Computer Configuration** | **Software Settings**) and right-click in the right pane to select **New** | **Package** from the context menu.

7. Navigate to the shared folder containing your package and select it. Click **Open**.

8. Select **Assigned** and click **OK** from the **Deployment** dialog box.

You can right-click on the newly created package to view its **Properties** and modify additional settings. For example, you may want to add a transformation file to the package (mst extension) to customize its behavior. You can also make sure it uninstalls automatically when it is no longer valid.

TIP   *You can also filter software installations with either security group. This lets you assign software installations through a single GPO while targeting different systems.*

To target a specific group with a software installation:

1. Locate the package you want to target (**GPO Editor** | **Computer Configuration** | **Software Settings** | **Software Installations**).

2. Right-click on the package and select **Properties**.

3. Move to the **Security** tab.

4. **Remove Authenticated Users** and add the appropriate group (this can be a global group containing only computer accounts) with **Read** rights.

5. Click **OK** to close the **Properties** dialog box.

Your installation will only be installed on the targeted group, because other systems will not be able to read it in the directory.

SCRIPT CENTER *The Microsoft TechNet Script Center includes three sample scripts that help you manage software installations. The first two install or remove software and the third lets you upgrade a software installation. These scripts can be found at http://www.microsoft.com/technet/treeview/default.asp?url=/technet/scriptcenter/compmgmt/default.asp?frame=true.*

DC-16: GPO Management

Activity Frequency: Ad hoc

Group Policy is one of the most powerful tools in Windows Server 2003. There are more than 900 GPO settings that can be applied in a Windows Server forest. These settings control everything from the appearance of a desktop to Terminal Service settings for all users. This is why you will be working with GPOs on a regular basis.

TIP *Be careful of how many GPOs you create. Avoid using single-purpose GPOs and use GPO filters to refine their application.*

1. Begin by launching the **Group Policy Management Console** portion of the Global MMC.

2. Navigate to the **Group Policy Objects** container (**Computer Management** | **Group Policy Management** | **Forest:** *forestname* | **Domains** | *domainname* | **Group Policy Objects**).

3. Locate the GPO to edit and right-click on it to select **Edit** from the context menu.

4. Perform the appropriate modification in the GPO Editor.

GPOs can be rapidly linked to any given container with the GPMC. To do so, drag and drop the GPO to the appropriate container.

GPOs can also be filtered. Two types of filters are available: security and Windows Management Instrumentation (WMI) filters. Security filters are simply access rights granted or denied to specific groups. WMI filters target specific results from a WMI query. For example, if all your portables are from Toshiba, you can use a WMI filter to target all Toshiba machines in your domain.

To apply filters to GPOs:

1. Begin by launching the **Group Policy Management Console** portion of the Global MMC.

2. Navigate to the **Group Policy Objects** container (**Computer Management** I **Group Policy Management** I **Forest:** *forestname* I **Domains** I *domainname* I **Group Policy Objects**).

3. Click the GPO to filter. In the right pane, add or remove security groups to filter the GPO with security.

4. To filter the GPO with a WMI query, click the drop-down list and select the appropriate filter. Answer **Yes** when queried by the **WMI Filter** dialog box. WMI filters must be created before you can apply them.

WMI filters are created by right-clicking on **WMI Filters** and selecting **New** from the context menu. WMI filters are comparable to SQL queries, though they use a different language: Windows Query Language (WQL). An example of a filter for locating Toshiba laptops is:

```
Root\CimV2; Select * from Win32_ComputerSystem
where manufacturer = "Toshiba" and Model =
"Satellite Pro 4200" OR Model = "Satellite Pro
4100"
```

WMI filters can be created in plaintext files and imported directly into the GPMC.

Finally, three GPO commands are really useful when working with Group Policy.

To update Group Policy on an object:

```
gpupdate
```

By default, this will update both the user and computer policies on the target system, but only changed settings. Use the /force switch to reapply all policy settings. Use /? for more information.

To identify the resulting set of policies on an object:

```
gpresult /S computername /USER targetusername /Z
```

where *computername* is the name of the computer to verify results on and *targetusername* is the name of the user whose policies you want to verify. The /Z switch enables super verbose mode, giving you highly detailed information. You might want to pipe this command into a filename to capture all the results.

To reset either the Default Domain or the Default Domain Controller GPO to its original setting:

```
dcgpofix /ignoreschema
```

By default, this command refreshes both default policies. The /ignoreschema switch is most certainly required if you have added any schema modifications or any schema-modifying software to your network. If the schema is no longer in its default state and the switch is not used, the command will not work.

DC-17: Computer Object Management

Activity Frequency: **Ad hoc**

All computer objects in Windows Server 2003 must have an account within the directory. This is because this account enables the directory to interact with each machine in the network. This is why machines must join an Active Directory domain. This join helps put in place all of the elements that support system management within AD.

There are two ways to create computer objects. First, they can be created during system staging when the computer's network parameters are defined, but using this method means granting the **Add workstation to domain** right to technicians. The second method allows you to precreate the computer accounts within the domain. The advantage of this method is that you can target the proper organizational unit for the computer account, making sure it benefits immediately from the GPO settings it requires.

To precreate a new computer object:

1. Launch the **Global MMC Console** (**Quick Launch Area** I **Global MMC Console**). The console automatically connects to your default domain. If you need to work with a different forest or domain controller, right-click on **Active Directory Users Computers** (**Computer Management** I **Active Directory Users and Computers**) and select the appropriate command to change your connection.

2. Navigate to the appropriate organizational unit (OU). If you are using the default Windows structure, this should be the Computers container (**Computer Management** I **Active Directory Users and Computers** I **domainname** I **Computers**).

TIP *The default Computers container in AD is not an organizational unit and therefore cannot support either delegation or the assignation of Group Policy Objects. GPOs must be assigned at the domain level to affect this container. If you want to assign GPOs to user objects but not at the domain level, you must create a new PCs OU.*

---

3. Either right-click in the right window pane to select the **New** I **Computer** command in the context menu or use the **New Computer** icon in the console toolbar. This activates the **New Object - Computer Wizard**.

4. This wizard displays two dialog boxes. The first deals with the account names. Here, you set the computer's name. You also have the opportunity to identify which user group can add this computer to a domain. To do so, click **Change**, type in the group name, click **Check Names**, select the right group, and click **OK**. Click **Next**.

SECURITY SCAN *You can create a Technicians group that can be assigned to this role. This way, you do not need to assign them any more rights than required.*

5. The second screen deals with the status of the computer in the directory. If the computer is a managed computer, you need to click **This is a managed computer** and type in its globally unique identifier (GUID). Click **Next**.

TIP *Every computer has a GUID. It can be found either in the computer's BIOS or on the computer's label along with its serial number. If you buy computers in bulk (as you should to avoid diversity as much as possible), you should get the manufacturer to provide you with a spreadsheet listing the GUID for each computer in the lot.*

6. Click **Finish** to create the account.

TIP *You should take the time to review and fill in the account's properties. It should at least be a member of the appropriate groups to receive the proper software installations (see **Procedure DC-15**).*

You can also automate the computer account creation process. The csvde command is designed to perform massive account modifications in AD. Use the following command to create multiple computer accounts at once:

```
csvde -i -f filename.csv -v -k
>outputfilename.txt
```

where -i turns on the import mode, -f indicates the source file for the import (*filename.csv*)—this source file must be in comma-separated value (CSV) format, -v puts the command in verbose mode, and -k tells it to ignore errors and continue to the end. You can review the *outputfilename.txt* file for the results of the operation.

TIP *If you receive spreadsheets containing machine GUIDs from your computer reseller, you can use these spreadsheets as the basis of your account creation comma-separated source file.*

SCRIPT CENTER *The Microsoft TechNet Script Center includes several sample scripts that help you manage computer accounts. These scripts can be found at http://www.microsoft.com/technet/treeview/ default.asp?url=/technet/scriptcenter/compmgmt/ default.asp?frame=true.*

DC-18: Distribution Group Management

Activity Frequency: **Ad hoc**

4

As mentioned in **Procedure DC-05**, distribution groups are designed to help regroup objects that don't need or don't support access rights. An excellent example of a distribution group is a mailing list of external contacts. Users can address the group name and automatically send an email to each member of the group.

TIP *Do not use distribution groups to duplicate security groups. Security groups have the same features as distribution groups and can also be used to target email.*

For this reason, these groups are used much less than security groups. Since there is no need to duplicate security groups for distribution purposes, you should have many fewer distribution groups than security groups.

Use **Procedure DC-05** and the logic in Figure 4-2 to create your distribution groups.

DC-19: AD Forest Management

Activity Frequency: **Ad hoc**

Forest administrators need to manage global activities within the forest. First and foremost, the forest administrator must authorize the creation of new forests, especially permanent forests. You should aim to limit the number of permanent forests in your network. This will help you control the total cost of ownership (TCO) of your network.

 **SECURITY SCAN** *Remember that each single instance of an Active Directory is a forest.*

Forests are created for the following reasons:

- **Different database schemas** Only one database structure can be stored within a single forest. If the schema must be different, it should be contained in a different forest. With the coming of Active Directory in Application Mode (AD/AM), there is little need to host multiple forests for schema reasons.

*TIP For more information on how AD/AM can help reduce the number of forests, see **Procedure DC-21**.*

- **Testing or development** If special testing is required—for example, for tools that will modify the schema of your production forest—you may need to create a testing forest. The same applies to development projects.

- **Perimeter forests** If your organization hosts an extranet or an Internet site, you may require a different forest to segregate and protect internal objects from the perimeter.

SECURITY SCAN *It is a very good idea to segregate internal forests from external perimeters. This way, you do not compromise internal security if your perimeter is attacked. You can use the Standard Edition of Microsoft MetaDirectory Services 2003 (MMS) to link information between the two forests. To download the Standard Edition of MMS, go to www.microsoft.com/download and search for it.*

You should also limit the number of domains contained within your forest. Both domains and forests should be justified before being created. The reasons for creating a domain include:

- **Different authentication rules** Domains form the boundary for the rules used to authenticate users and computers since they are the container in which these objects are created.

- **Different security policies for user accounts** Security policies applying to user accounts are stored within the domain. These may need to be different from one domain to another. For example, developers usually require more elevated privileges than normal users. It is a good idea to let developers work in separate domains to avoid security compromises in your production domain.

- **Different publication services for shared resources** All of the resources that can be shared within a domain are published through Active Directory. By default, these resources—shared printers and folders—are published only to members of the domain. You may justify a different domain to protect critical resources.

Forest administrators must authorize child domain creation before these domains can be staged. Use the following commands to preauthorize a child domain in the directory:

```
ntdsutil
domain management
precreate domainDN firstdcname
quit
quit
```

where *domainDN* is the distinguished name for the child domain (for example, for the test.tandt.net domain, dc=test,dc=tandt,dc=net) and *firstdcname* is the fully qualified DNS name for the server that will be hosting the creation of the child domain. You must also delegate domain creation rights to the administrator performing the DC promotion. Use **Procedure DC-14** to do so.

TIP   Refer to **Procedure DN-04** *to properly prestage the DNS zone and application partition for this child domain.*

DC-20: AD Information Management

Activity Frequency: Ad hoc

Contrary to Windows NT's Security Account Manager (SAM), Active Directory thrives on information. For example, when you publish a shared folder in the directory (see **Procedure FS-03**), you should take the time to identify the folder's owner in the directory. This way, if you have problems with the folder, you know whom to contact. The same goes for adding user information or identifying group managers. The more information you put in the directory, the easier it will be to manage. You can use **Procedures DC-01** and **DC-05** to add both additional user information and group managers, but you can also use massive information management methods to add missing information.

For example, **Procedure DC-01** outlines how to use the `csvde` command to add several users at once. This tool can also be used to add more information when you create groups and other object types.

TIP   If you choose to add more information such as group managers and shared folder owners, you will have to make sure you do not delete accounts when users leave or change position. If you do so, you will have to modify ownership in each object, whereas if you simply rename existing accounts and reassign them, they will remain in all directory locations.

SCRIPT CENTER   The Microsoft TechNet Script Center includes several sample scripts that help you manage AD information. These scripts can be found at http://www.microsoft.com/technet/treeview/ default.asp?url=/technet/scriptcenter/user/ default.asp?frame=true.

DC-21: Schema Management

✔ Activity Frequency: Ad hoc

The Active Directory schema defines the structure of a forest database. By default, the Windows Server 2003 schema contains over 200 different object types and over 1,000 attributes. The AD schema is extensible; it allows you to add new structures to the database so that you may add content of your choice. Several tools can be used to extend the schema, but before you do so, you should ask yourself if it is really necessary.

The AD database is a distributed database. This means that it is spread out throughout your organization, often having domain controllers in each regional office as well as in the central ones. This means that each time you change the AD schema, it will be replicated to all locations. Another factor that should dampen your desire to change the schema is that changes cannot be undone. Though you can deactivate new object classes or attributes added to the schema, you cannot delete them. You can, however, rename and reuse them.

With Windows 2000, this was a significant dilemma, but it is not so with Windows Server 2003 because it supports Active Directory in Application Mode (AD/AM). AD/AM is like a mini-AD that can run several instances on a single machine (Windows XP or Windows Server). This means that instead of planning to modify your network operating system (NOS) AD, you should always consider the possibility of replacing this modification with an AD/AM instance. This will maintain your NOS AD in the most pristine version possible.

TIP To download AD/AM, go to www.microsoft.com/download and search for it.

There will, however, be some instances when schema modification is a must. This mostly relates to NOS-related tools such as quota management or AD management, or even add-ons such as Systems Management Server or Microsoft Exchange. Exchange, for example, more than doubles the number of objects and attributes in the NOS schema. In this case, use **Procedures DC-22** and **DC-23** to do so.

But, if you do decide to modify the schema, it should be done according to a schema modification policy. This policy includes:

- A detailed list of the members of the Enterprise Administrators universal group.

- A security and management strategy for the Schema Administrators universal group (see **Procedure DC-22**).

- The creation of the schema change policy holder (SCPH) role. This role is responsible for the approval or denial of all schema changes.

- Complete documentation of the schema change management strategy, including:

  - Supporting change request documentation, which provides a description and justification for the desired modification.

  - An impact analysis for the change; short-term and long-term replication impacts; costs for the requested change; short-term and long-term benefits for the change.

  - A globally unique object identifier for the new class or attribute obtained from a valid source (see **Procedure DC-23**).

  - An official class description, including class type and localization in the hierarchy.

  - Test results for system stability and security. Design a standard set of tests for all modifications.

  - A documented modification recovery method. Ensure every modification proposal includes a rollback strategy.

- A modification authorization process—this describes the meeting structure you use to review a recommendation for modification.

- A modification implementation process outlining when the change should be performed (off production hours), how it should be performed, and by whom.

- A modification report documentation. Did the modification reach all DCs? Is replication back to expected levels?

Modifying the schema is a process that has significant impact. It should not be taken lightly.

4

DC-22: Schema Access Management

Activity Frequency: Ad hoc

Windows Server includes two universal administration groups: Enterprise Administrators and Schema Administrators. Enterprise Administrators are the forest managers. They are responsible for the overall operation of the forest. This is an ongoing task.

 **SECURITY SCAN**   *Schema Administrators are not operational in that they are only required when a modification is performed on the schema. This should be a rare occasion at best. It is therefore a security best practice to keep the Schema Administrators group empty at all times.*

In fact, your security and management strategy for the Schema Administrators universal group should be focused on keeping this group empty. Members should be added only when a modification is required and removed once the modification has been performed.

TIP All schema modifications must be performed directly on the schema operations master.

 **SECURITY SCAN**   *You must be a member of the Enterprise Administrators group to perform this procedure.*

Use the following procedure to control schema access:

1. Use **Procedure DC-05** to add an authorized user to the Schema Administrators group. This procedure must be performed in the root domain of your forest.

2. Allow the authorized user to perform the modification.

3. Use **Procedure DC-05** to remove the user from the Schema Administrators group.

TIP   All schema modifications should be fully tested in a laboratory environment before being performed in the production network.

DC-23: Schema Content Modification

Activity Frequency: Ad hoc

The best way to protect your production schema is to formulate a schema modification policy (see **Procedure DC-21**). This policy is upheld by a schema change policy holder (SCPH) to whom all schema changes are presented for approval. The policy will outline not only who holds the SCPH role, but also how schema modifications are to be tested, prepared, and deployed. Assigning the SCPH role to manage the schema ensures that modifications will not be performed on an ad hoc basis by groups that do not communicate with each other. Since all modifications must be approved by the SCPH first and foremost, the process is clear for everyone.

The X.500 structure of the AD database is based on an object numbering scheme that is globally unique. Thus a central authority has the ability to generate object identifiers for new X.500 objects: the International Standards Organization (ISO). Numbers can also be obtained from the American National Standards Institute (ANSI). As such, X.500 numbering can be obtained at http://www.iso.org or http://www.ansi.org. Microsoft also offers X.500 numbering in an object class tree it acquired for the purpose of supporting Active Directory. You can receive object IDs from Microsoft by sending email to *oids@microsoft.com*. In your email, include your organization's naming prefix, and the following information: contact name, contact address, and contact telephone number. To obtain your organization's naming prefix, read the Active Directory portion of the Logo standards at http://www.microsoft.com/winlogo/downloads/software.asp.

Object identifiers are strings in a dot notation similar to IP addresses. Issuing authorities can give an object identifier on a sublevel to other authorities. The ISO is the root authority. The ISO has a number of 1. When it assigns a number to another organization, that number is used to identify that organization. If it assigned an organization the number 488077, and it issued 1 to a developer, and that developer assigned 10 to an application, the number of the application would be "1.488077.1.10."

Object identifiers are required each time you want to add an object or attribute to the AD schema. Obtain these identifiers before you proceed to modify the schema.

Schema modifications do not only reside with object or attribute additions. You can modify the schema to:

- Add an object or attribute to the Global Catalog. This makes it available to all users in your organization.

- Index an object within the directory. This renders the object searchable.

- Deactivate an object or attribute. This makes the object dormant in your directory. Only objects you added to the directory can be deactivated.

- Rename and reuse an added object or attribute.

Modifications can be performed interactively, through command-line tools or through programming. To modify the directory schema interactively:

1. Make sure you have been added to the Schema Administrators group (see **Procedure DC-22**).

2. Register the schema management DLL on your computer:

```
regsvr32 schmmgmt.dll
```

3. Click **OK** when the **regsvr32** dialog box tells you the DLL has been successfully registered.

4. Use **Procedure GS-17** to add the **AD Schema Management** snap-in to your Global MMC.

5. In the Global MMC, right-click on the **Active Directory Schema** and select **Change Domain Controller**. Select **Specify Name**, type in the DNS name of your Schema Operations Master, and then click **OK**.

6. Click **Active Directory Schema** to display its contents.

7. To create a class or an attribute, right-click on either and select **Create Class** or **Create Attribute** from the context menu. Windows Server will give you a warning about the permanency of this operation. Proceed with care.

8. To modify any of the existing classes or attributes, right-click on the object and select **Properties**. Select the appropriate property to modify and click **OK** when done.

9. To deactivate or rename classes or attributes you have already added, right-click on the appropriate object and select the proper command from the context menu. Proceed with care.

10. Make note of any changes you make and notify the Enterprise Administrator when you have completed your operation so that your account can be removed from the Schema Administrators group.

You can also use several other tools for more massive schema modifications. For example, the ldifde command provides a structured way to modify the schema through the command line. Type ldifde /? at the command prompt for more information.

TIP   *If you decide to modify your schema anyway, you can document your modifications through a schema documentation program available from the Microsoft download web site. Search for schema documentation program at www.microsoft.com/downloads.*

DC-24: Schema-Modifying Software Evaluation

Activity Frequency: Ad hoc

Both Microsoft and third-party manufacturers use schema extensions to more fully integrate their products to Active Directory. Microsoft Exchange is the one product that makes the most modifications to the schema because it almost doubles its structure.

4

You should be wary of schema-modifying software because it has a very long-term impact on your NOS directory. Remember that the directory you create in your network will last a long time and will need to be easily upgradeable when new versions of Windows Server products come out.

When you need to decide if you will proceed with a given product that modifies the schema, you should take the following elements into consideration:

- What is the reputation and financial livelihood of the product's manufacturer? You do not want to find yourself bound to a product that no longer has support after you have implemented it.

- Is the function the product provides truly essential? Are there other products on the market that perform the same function without modifying the schema?

- What is the manufacturer's approach to Active Directory in Application Mode? Have they committed to AD/AM integration instead of NOS directory modifications?

The answer to these questions will help you determine if you should implement the product or not. Of course, in some cases, the question doesn't really pose itself. For example, if your organization is running Exchange and migrated to Windows Server, you won't think twice about modifying the schema.

Once your decision is made to go forward, rely on **Procedures DC-21**, **DC-22**, and **DC-23** to perform the modification.

DC-25: Operations Master Role Management

Activity Frequency: Ad hoc

Operations Master roles are AD services that manage requests for specific information changes at either the forest or the domain level. Without these services, AD cannot operate. They fall into two groups: forest-wide and domain-centric Operations Master roles. The Operations Master role is sometimes called flexible single master of operations (FSMO) because even though only a single instance can exist in the forest or the domain, this instance is not rooted to a given server; it can be transferred from one domain controller to another. Thus, it is flexible and it is single because it must be unique within its scope of influence.

Forest-wide Operations Master roles are:

- **Schema Master** The master service that maintains the structure of the forest database and authorizes schema changes.

- **Domain Naming Master** The master service that controls and authorizes domain naming within the forest.

Only a single instance of these services can exist in the forest at a given time. Both services can be located on the same domain controller if required. In large forests, these services are distributed on two separate domain controllers.

In addition to forest-wide Operations Master roles, there are domain-centric Operations Master roles. If you only have one domain in your forest, you will have a single instance of each of these roles, but if you have more than one domain, every domain will have one instance of each of these services. These include:

- **Relative ID (RID) Master** The master service that is responsible for the assignation of relative IDs to other domain controllers within the domain. Whenever a new object—user, computer, server, or group—is created within a domain, the domain controller who is performing the creation will assign a unique ID number. This ID number consists of a domain identification number followed by a relative identification number that is assigned at object creation. When a domain controller runs out of its pool of relative IDs, it requests an additional pool from the RID Master. The relative ID role is also the placeholder for the domain. If you need to move objects between domains in the same forest, you need to initiate the move from the RID Master.

- **Primary Domain Controller (PDC) Emulator** The master service that provides backward compatibility for Windows NT. If there are Windows NT domain controllers or Windows NT network clients within the domain, this server acts as the primary domain controller for the domain. It manages all replication to backup domain controllers (in NT, of course). If the forest operates in native mode, the PDC Emulator focuses on its two other roles: Time Synchronization on all DCs and computers, and Preferential Account Modification Replication to other DCs. All domain controllers in the domain will set their clock according to the PDC Emulator. In addition, any account modification that is critical, such as password modification or account deactivation, will be immediately replicated to the PDC Emulator from the originating server. If a logon attempt fails on a given DC, it checks with the PDC Emulator before rejecting the attempt because it may not have received recent password changes.

- **Infrastructure Master** The master service that manages two critical tasks. The update of references from objects in its domain to objects in other domains. This is how the forest knows to which domain an object belongs. The Infrastructure Master has a close relationship to the Global Catalog (GC). If it finds that some of its objects are out-of-date compared to the GC, it will request an update from the GC and send the updated information to other DCs within the domain. For this reason, the Global Catalog Service should not be on a DC acting as the Infrastructure Master. The Infrastructure Master also manages the update and modification of group members within the domain. If a group includes objects from another domain and these objects are renamed or moved, the Infrastructure Master will maintain the consistency of the group and replicate it to all other domain controllers. This ensures that users maintain access rights even though you perform maintenance operations on their accounts.

The domain-centric master roles should be separated if possible. This depends, of course, on the size of each domain. Whatever its size, each domain should have at least two domain controllers for redundancy, load balancing, and availability.

Operations Master roles can be managed both graphically or through the command line. The three domain-centric master roles can be identified through the Active Directory Users and Computers console by right-clicking on the domain name and selecting **Properties**. In the Domain Properties dialog box, use the appropriate tab to identify the DC holding each role. The forest-wide master roles are more independent. Use the Active Directory Domains and Trusts console to find the Domain Naming Master. Once again, right-click on the domain name and select **Operations Master**. To find the Schema Master, use the AD Schema console created in **Procedure DC-23**.

The easiest way to find Operations Master roles is through the command line:

```
dsquery server -hasfsmo fsmoname
```

This command works for each of the five roles. The *fsmoname* for each role is as follows: name for the Domain Naming Master, infr for the Infrastructure Master, pdc for the PDC Emulator, rid for the RID Master, and schema for the Schema Master.

SCRIPT CENTER *The Microsoft TechNet Script Center includes a sample script that helps you identify FSMO roles. This script can be found at http:// www.microsoft.com/technet/treeview/default.asp?url=/ technet/scriptcenter/compmgmt/ScrCM24.asp?frame=true.*

DC-26: Operations Master Role Transfer

Activity Frequency: **Ad hoc**

As you know, there can only be a single instance of each Operations Master role within each scope, forest, or domain. While, in most cases, the forest or domain will operate for short periods of time when one or the other master is down, it is preferable to transfer the role from one DC to another if you know that one of the Operations Master DCs will be down for significant periods of time. This can happen when maintenance is scheduled on the server.

4

TIP   *Transferring Operations Master roles can be dangerous to your production network if not performed properly. For example, transferring the Schema Master role improperly can damage the entire forest schema, forcing you to recover Active Directory from backups. Be sure you perform these operations carefully.*

To transfer any of the roles through the graphical interface, you basically need to use the FSMO's identification procedure as outlined in **Procedure DC-25**. Here's how:

1. Launch the appropriate console for the FSMO you want to transfer.

2. Right-click on the domain name and select **Connect to a Domain Controller**, type in the name of the DC you want to transfer the role to, and click **OK**.

3. View the **FSMO Properties** dialog box and click **Change**.

Once again, it is easier to do so through the command line:

```
ntdsutil
roles
connection
connect to server servername
quit
transfer FSMOname
quit
quit
```

where *servername* is the DNS name for the DC you want to transfer the role to and *FSMOname* is the role you want to transfer. Type `help` at the `fsmo maintenance` prompt to identify FSMO names for this command.

DC-27: Operations Master Disaster Recovery

Activity Frequency: Ad hoc

Procedure DC-26 only works when the FSMO you want to transfer is still operating. In the case of a total systems failure of an FSMO, you need to seize the FSMO role; that is, you need to tell the directory that the role must be transferred even if it cannot contact the originating FSMO.

TIP *Do not seize any role if it can be transferred instead. The seizure operation does not remove the role from the originating server. The operation of two FSMOs with the same role in the same domain or forest can severely damage the directory.*

Role seizure is performed through the `ntdsutil` command:

```
ntdsutil
roles
connection
connect to server servername
quit
seize FSMOname
quit
quit
```

where *servername* is the DNS name for the DC you want to seize the role to and *FSMOname* is the role you want to seize. Type `help` at the `fsmo maintenance` prompt to identify FSMO names for this command.

TIP *If you seize any role, make sure the role is completely removed from the originating server before bringing it back online in the forest or domain. If not, there can be serious damage to your Active Directory.*

DC-28: Domain Controller Promotion

Activity Frequency: **Ad hoc**

Domain controllers in Windows Server 2003 are much different than in Windows NT. In Windows Server, you can easily switch a server from DC to member server and back if you want to. All is done through the `DCPromo` command. This command can be accessed through a variety of methods: command line, Manage Your Server (MYS) interface, `run` command, and so on. The easiest is through the MYS interface. This is launched automatically at system startup or through **Start Menu | Administrative Tools**.

The promotion of a domain controller can be done in a number of different situations. It can be for the creation of a new forest. In this instance, you tell DCPromo that you want to install the first DC in a forest. It can be for a new tree in an existing forest. It can be for a child domain. It can also be for another DC in an existing domain.

SECURITY SCAN   *To use DCPromo, you either need to have Enterprise or Domain Administrator rights or to have the appropriate delegated rights. Delegated rights must be provided in conjunction with **Procedure DC-19** if your intent is to create a new child domain or tree in an existing forest.*

*TIP   If you are creating a child domain in an existing forest, you must perform **Procedure DN-04** before running DCPromo.*

To run DCPromo from the MYS interface:

1. Click **Add or remove a role**. This will launch the Configure Your Server Wizard.

2. Review the configuration requirements and then click **Next**. Windows Server 2003 will verify the existing roles on the server and produce a selection of installation options.

3. Select **Domain Controller (Active Directory)** and then click **Next**. Confirm your selection by clicking **Next**. This launches the Active Directory Installation Wizard. Click **Next**.

4. The selection you make here determines which type of DC you are creating. Choose the appropriate selection and click **Next**. The selection you make will condition the behavior of the Active Directory Installation Wizard.

5. Whichever your selection, you will need to name the domain you are creating or within which your DC is being integrated, give its NetBIOS name, select the location of the database and log folders, and select the location of the SYSVOL folder (replication folder).

6. If you are creating a new domain, the AD Installation Wizard will try to find a DNS record for the domain. The preferred behavior is that the Wizard return an error code, because this forces it to prompt for the installation of the DNS service. In all instances, you should select **Install and Configure the DNS server**, then click **Next** to launch the DNS installation process.

7. If you are creating a new domain, the next question will relate to the default permission level for users and groups. If you intend to run pre-Windows 2000 operating systems within this network, you need to set these permissions now. It is preferable to select the second option, **Permissions compatible with only Windows 2000 or Windows Server 2003 operating systems**.

8. You will also need to set the **Directory Service Restore Mode Administrator Password**. This password is extremely important since it is the password used to perform authoritative restores or restores that overwrite existing directory information during system recovery (see **Procedure DC-29**). Guard it carefully.

9. The DC Promotion service will outline your choices—review them carefully and, when ready to proceed, click **Next**. This will launch the Active Directory Installation Wizard. It will perform a series of tasks,

including the reapplication of security parameters on the server's disks, and it will launch the DNS installation process.

TIP *If you are creating a new domain, the Windows Server installation files will be required to perform the installation of the DNS service.*

10. Once complete, the AD Installation Wizard displays a completion report. Click **Finish**. The system will require a restart to finalize the AD installation operation. Once the system has restarted and initialized the Active Directory, the Configure Your Server Wizard displays a completion page after you log on.

4

When creating regional domains, it is useful to preload the directory information during the DC promotion. This greatly reduces replication requirements since only the differences between the actual directory and the backup from which the preload is performed are replicated.

TIP *Before you can promote a DC using preloaded information, you must use* **Procedures BR-01** *to create a system state backup from a DC in the target domain, and* **BR-05** *to restore the data on the member server being promoted. Use* **Restore files to: Alternate location** *to restore the system state data on the member server.*

To perform the DC promotion from backup files, use:

```
dcpromo /adv
```

DC-29: Domain Controller Disaster Recovery

Activity Frequency: Ad hoc

With the reliability of today's server hardware, especially brand name server hardware, it is rare to completely lose a DC, but it does happen often enough to have to use a disaster recovery procedure on DCs. There are three types of DC disaster recovery operations: nonauthoritative, authoritative, and primary.

The first is the simplest. It implies that the DC that was lost did not have any unreplicated data within its directory store. When this is the case, you can simply rebuild the server, perform **Procedure DC-28** to rebuild the DC with or without backup data, and let AD replication do the rest. It will automatically bring the server up-to-date.

If there was lost data or if there was a major data loss within the directory and you must perform an authoritative restore, you must use the ntdsutil tool to make the restore authoritative. To perform an authoritative restore, you must begin with a normal restore. Then, once the data is restored and the domain controller is still offline, you enter ntdsutil to finish the job. The authoritative restore can include all or just a portion of the restored AD data:

1. Repair the server, if required, and start it up. During startup, press F8 to view the startup modes.

2. Select the **Directory Services Restore Mode** and press ENTER.

3. This will boot into Windows. Log in with the directory restore account. Launch the backup utility and perform the restore. Once the restoration is finished, reboot the server.

4. Press F8 once again to select **Directory Services Restore Mode** and press ENTER. Log in with the directory restore account. Launch the command prompt:

```
ntdsutil
authoritative restore
restore database
quit
quit
```

5. Restart the server in normal mode.

The restore database command marks all of the data in the NTDS.DIT database of this DC as authoritative. Once the server is restarted, the replication process will start and the restored information will be replicated to all other domain controllers.

If you want to restore only a portion of the directory, use the following `restore` command:

```
restore subtree ou=ouname,dc=dcname,dc=dcname
```

where you must supply the distinguished name of the OU you want to restore.

The last restore type is the primary restore. It is used when all the DCs for a domain are lost and you need to rebuild a domain.

4

TIP *Given that you should always have at least two DCs in any domain, you should rarely have to use this procedure.*

If you do have to use this procedure, you must rebuild the server. Use **Procedure DC-28** to promote the server to DC status and then use restart in Directory Services Restore Mode (see above). Once the server is restarted, use **Procedure BR-05** to restore System State Data to the server. Make sure you access the Advanced features of the restore to select **When restoring replicated data sets, mark the restored data as the primary data for all replicas** in the Advanced Restore wizard's third screen.

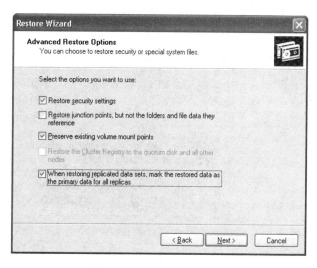

Reboot the server once the restore is complete. This should recover the primary DC for the lost domain.

DC-30: Trust Management

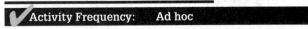

Activity Frequency: Ad hoc

Windows Server 2003 forests automatically include transitive trusts between all of their domains. These trusts must operate properly for the forest to operate properly. These trusts support the operation of the forest through forest-wide replication, which includes the content of the Global Catalog, the schema, and the forest configuration.

If you are within a very large forest and there is a significant amount of interdomain operational activity, you may also consider the creation of shortcut trusts—manual trusts that are created to link two domains in a forest. The shortcut trust speeds operation because communications do not need to go through the forest hierarchy. In fact, Windows Server forests support several different types of trusts (see Table 4-3).

Trust Type	Directions and Nature	Comments
Parent and Child	Two-way transitive	These are the automatic trusts that are established when a child domain is created.
Tree-root	Two-way transitive	These are the automatic trusts that are established when a new tree is created.
Forest	One- or two-way transitive	Extends the transitivity of trusts from one forest to another.
Shortcut	One- or two-way transitive	Creates a shortcut path for authentication between two domains. The domains can use this path for authentication instead of having to traverse the forest hierarchy.

Table 4-3. Windows Server Trust Types

Trust Type	Directions and Nature	Comments
Realm	One- or two-way transitive or nontransitive	Creates an authentication link between a domain and a non-Windows Kerberos realm (such as UNIX).
External	One- or two-way nontransitive	Creates an authentication link between a Windows Server domain and an NT4 domain.

Table 4-3. Windows Server Trust Types *(continued)*

The first two trust types listed in Table 4-3 are created automatically when you use **Procedure DC-28** to create a new child domain or tree in a forest. The others are created manually to either improve performance or to enable interaction between one authentication zone and another.

SECURITY SCAN *Trust operations require high privileges. This means either Domain or Enterprise Administrators (depending on the level of trust required). You will also need privileged credentials in the target domain, especially if you are creating two-way transitive trusts.*

To create a trust:

1. Move to the **Active Directory Domains and Trusts** section of the Global MMC.

2. Right-click on the domain you want to assign the trust to and select **Properties**.

3. Move to the **Trust** tab in the **Properties** dialog box and click **New Trust**. This will launch the New Trust Wizard. Click **Next**.

4. Type in the name of the domain or forest you wish to establish the trust with. Domain names can be in NetBIOS format, but forest names must be in DNS format. Click **Next**.

5. Select the type of trust you wish to create (two-way, one-way: incoming, or one-way: outgoing).

6. If you have administrative rights in both domains, you can select **Both this domain and the specified domain** to create both sides of the trust at the same time. Click **Next**.

7. Type in your administrative credentials for the target domain or forest. Click **Next**.

8. The wizard is ready to create the outgoing trust in the target domain or forest. Click **Next**. Once finished, it will ask you to configure the new trust. Click **Next**.

9. Select **Yes, confirm the outgoing trust** and then click **Next**. Confirming trusts is a good idea because it tests the new trust immediately.

10. Select **Yes, confirm the incoming trust** and then click **Next**. Review your changes and click **Finish** when done.

SECURITY SCAN *If you do not have credentials for both domains, you must run the New Trust Wizard once in each domain. In this case, you must provide the same trust password each time. It is a good idea to use very strong passwords for trust relationships. This means complex passwords that have at least 15 characters.*

Use the same procedure to create all other types of trusts. The wizard will automatically change its behavior based on the values you input in its second page.

To verify trusts:

1. Move to the **Active Directory Domains and Trusts** section of the Global MMC.

2. Right-click on the domain containing the trusts on which you want to verify trust and select **Properties**.

3. Move to the **Trust** tab in the **Properties** dialog box and click on **Select the trust you want to verify (either incoming or outgoing)**. Click **Properties**.

4. Click **Validate**. In the **Validate Trust** dialog box, determine if you want to validate the trust in both directions (if it is a two-way trust) and click **OK**.

SECURITY SCAN   *If you verify two-way trusts in both directions, you need proper credentials in the target domain.*

To verify trusts at the command line:

```
netdom trust trustingdomainname /
d:trusteddomainname /verify
```

where the domain names must be in DNS format. If the trust is a two-way trust, you will need to provide proper credentials for the target domain.

4

SCRIPT CENTER   *The Microsoft TechNet Script Center includes two sample scripts that help you manage trusts. The first lets you identify trust relationships and the second lets you configure trust properties. These scripts can be found at http:// www.microsoft.com/technet/treeview/default.asp?url=/ technet/scriptcenter/monitor/default.asp?frame=true.*

DC-31: Forest/Domain/ OU Structure Management

✓ Activity Frequency: Ad hoc

Active Directory is a truly virtual environment. This means that there are a lot of restructuring options available in AD. Your forest or domain structure does not necessarily need to be absolutely final when you put it in place. Of course, you try to plan in the most effective manner possible when you first prepare your AD, but you will most likely discover that as you become familiar with AD, you will want to improve upon your original design. Windows Server offers several tools for domain or forest restructuring:

- The Active Directory Users and Computers console fully supports drag and drop. Therefore, it is relatively simple to restructure the contents of a single domain by dragging and dropping objects such as users, computers, and even organizational units from one place to another. You can even search for objects containing given characteristics and move them all at once. Be sure to use **Procedure DC-16** to verify GPO links after any OU restructuring activity.

- The `MoveTree` command is the command-line equivalent of the Active Directory Users and Computers console. It provides more functionality because it will move objects between domains in the same forest—something the console cannot do.

- You can also use the `RenDom` command to rename domains (found under the Valueadd\Msft\Mgmt\ Domren folder of the Windows Server CD). This command is useful for supporting forest restructuring during corporate merges or acquisitions, or during reorganizations. You can even use this tool to rename an entire forest, one domain at a time.

- The Active Directory Migration Tool supports massive object moves either within forests or between forests, even NT domains (found under the i386\ADMT folder of the Windows Server CD). This powerful tool gives you greater flexibility during large reorganizations.

TIP *The last two tools are fairly complex and require significant testing before you proceed. Be sure to become thoroughly familiar with these tools before using them in a production environment. For example, if you use the Rename Domain tool improperly, your domain could become corrupt, forcing you to recover it from backups.*

The `MoveTree` command lets you move objects and track the movements by piping the information into archivable record files. In addition, it includes a `/check` switch that will only test the move before actually performing the operation. Included with the `/verbose` switch, this will give you a lot of information about the potential move before you actually perform it. Also, by default, the `/start` switch will automatically verify a move and perform the move only if the verification operation completes without errors. For example, to test a move of the HR OU into the Admin OU from Server1 to Server2 in the TandT.net domain and pipe the results into a file, type:

```
movetree /check /s server1.tandt.net /d
server2.tandt.net /sdn OU=HR,DC=tandt,DC=net /
ddn OU=HR,OU=Admin,DC=tandt,DC=net /verbose
>filename.txt
```

Use `movetree /?` for more information.

TIP   Remember that organizational units are used for four reasons: to delegate object administration, to assign Group Policies to objects, to regroup or categorize objects, and to hide objects. The latter is performed through the assignation or denial of read permissions to the OU. Use **Procedure DC-34** to assign appropriate permissions to OUs.

SCRIPT CENTER   The Microsoft TechNet Script Center includes several sample scripts that help you manage OUs. These scripts can be found at http://www.microsoft.com/technet/treeview/default.asp?url=/technet/scriptcenter/user/default.asp?frame=true.

DC-32: Active Directory Script Management

Activity Frequency: **Ad hoc**

Procedure GS-08 shows how to use the WMI Scriptomatic utility to generate WMI scripts. The Microsoft TechNet Script Center also provides a version of Scriptomatic that works with the Active Directory Services Interface (ADSI). ADSI Scriptomatic is available from the Microsoft Download Center. Just search for ADSI Scriptomatic at www.microsoft.com/downloads.

Installing ADSI Scriptomatic is simply a matter of unzipping the file from the downloaded compressed archive. You should store the EZADscriptomatic.hta file in the C:\ToolKit folder. You can also use a Run As shortcut (see **Procedure GS-01**) to execute EZAD Scriptomatic and place it in the Quick Launch Area.

To write a script with EZAD Scriptomatic:

1. Launch **EZADscriptomatic.hta** or your **Run As** shortcut.

2. In EZAD Scriptomatic, select the action you want to perform from the **Select a task** drop-down list. Four tasks are available: Create, Write, Read, and Delete an object.

3. Next, select the type of object you want to affect from the **Select a class** drop-down list. For example, to write a script that lets you create a computer account, first select **Create an object** and then select the **Computer** class. EZAD Scriptomatic automatically generates the proper script (see Figure 4-3).

TIP *EZAD Scriptomatic cannot create personalized scripts because it does not know your particular AD. You must modify the object names in order to personalize them before running any script created by EZAD Scriptomatic. For more information, click* **Read this before running the create an object–computer script**.

4. Modify both the strContainer and strName values. For example to create a computer account named PC_HQ_001 in the Managed OU under the PCs top level OU, use the following values:

```
strContainer="ou=Managed,ou=PCs"
strName="PC_HQ_001"
```

5. Click **Run**. EZAD Scriptomatic will launch a command console to run the script.

6. Click **Save** to save the script to a file (VBS extension).

You can use these scripts to perform administrative tasks and capture the output. To do so, use the following command:

```
cscript scriptname.vbs >filename.txt
```

where *scriptname.vbs* is the name of the script you want to run and *filename.txt* is the name of the output file you want to create.

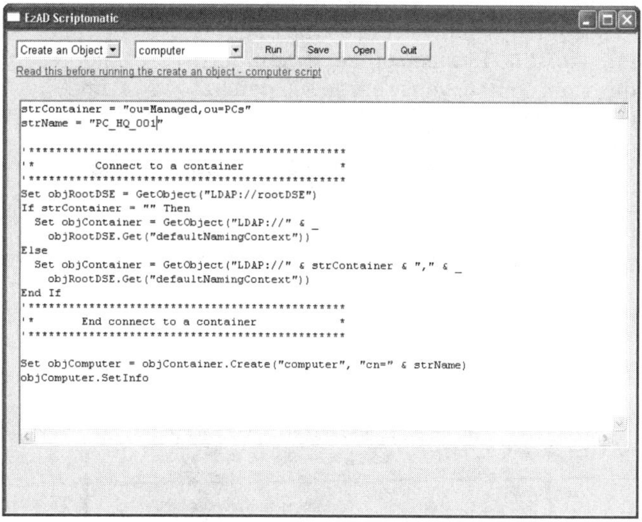

Figure 4-3. To generate a script that creates a computer account, select **Create an object** and the **computer** class in EZAD Scriptomatic.

DC-33: Forest Time Service Management

Activity Frequency: Ad hoc

Active Directory includes a time synchronization hierarchy. This hierarchy is based on the PDC Emulator within each domain of the forest. The forest root domain PDC Emulator is normally synchronized with an external time source and each child domain PDC emulator synchronizes with the PDC Emulator from the forest root domain. Each computer or server in each domain synchronizes with its own PDC Emulator.

Time synchronization in Windows Server is managed in two ways: The first is through the w32tm command. This command lets you control time on individual computers. The second is through the domain hierarchy. If you wish to use alternate times sources, Windows Server includes several GPOs that let you control time globally within domains.

By default, Windows Server 2003 networks are configured to use time.windows.com as the Simple Network Time Protocol (SNTP) time source. If your network cannot reach this time source, your server will generate W32Time errors such as error number 12.

If you wish to set a different time source server for the forest root PDC Emulator, use the w32tm command-line tool. For example, the command to use to set an Eastern time zone clock with three source time servers would be:

```
w32tm /config /
manualpeerlist:"ntp2.usno.navy.mil,
tick.usno.navy.mil, tock.usno.navy.mil" /
update
```

This will set the forest root PDC Emulator to synchronize time with one of the three computer systems listed and it will immediately update the time service. Remember, to do this, you will have to open UDP port 123 in your firewall to allow SNTP traffic. Use Table 4-4 to identify an appropriate time source for your network.

To verify that the command was successful, type:

```
net time /querysntp
```

This should return the three new time sources as the result.

***

TIP *A list of nonmilitary public time servers is available at http://www.eecis.udel.edu/~mills/ntp/clock1a.html.*

There is no need to configure GPOs for time synchronization, because every computer joined to a domain automatically obtains its time settings from the PDC Emulator.

Time Zone	Available Addresses
U.S. Eastern Time Zone	ntp2.usno.navy.mil
	tick.usno.navy.mil
	tock.usno.navy.mil
	ntp-s1.cise.ufl.edu
	ntp.colby.edu
	navobs1.oar.net
	gnomon.cc.columbia.edu
	tick.gatech.edu
	navobs1.mit.edu
U.S. Central Time Zone	now.cis.okstate.edu
	ntp0.mcs.anl.gov
	navobs1.wustl.edu
	tick.uh.edu
U.S. Mountain Time Zone	tick.usnogps.navy.mil
	tock.usnogps.navy.mil
U.S. Pacific Time Zone	montpelier.caltech.edu
	bigben.cac.washington.edu
	tick.ucla.edu
	usno.pa-x.dec.com
Alaska Time Zone	ntp.alaska.edu
Hawaii Time Zone	tick.mhpcc.edu

Table 4-4. US Naval Observatory Master Clock Addresses (http://tycho.usno.navy.mil/ntp.html)

DC-34: Access Control List Management

Activity Frequency: Ad hoc

One of the reasons you use organizational units is to hide objects in the directory. Since users have the ability to query the directory, it is a good idea to hide sensitive objects such as service or administrative accounts.

SECURITY SCAN *This should be taken as a security best practice. The first part of hacking is having the information on hand. If you hide the information by applying access control lists to OUs, you will have a more secure network.*

---

*TIP Before performing this task, use **Procedure DC-05** to create a security group called **Denied Users** and assign all users from whom you want to hide information to this group. Make sure you do not include your administrative accounts in this group; otherwise, you will also be denied access to the hidden information.*

To secure the contents of an OU:

1. Launch the **Global MMC (Quick Launch Area | Global MMC)** and move to **Active Directory Users and Computers (Computer Management | Active Directory Users and Computers)**.

2. Expand the domain name and either move to, or create, the OU you want to modify. To create an OU, right-click on the parent object (domain or parent OU) and select **New | Organizational Unit**.

3. Right-click on the OU and select **Properties** from the context menu.

4. Move to the **Security** tab. Click **Add**. Type **Denied Users** and click **OK**.

5. Assign the **Deny Read** permission to the Denied Users group. Click **OK** to close the dialog box.

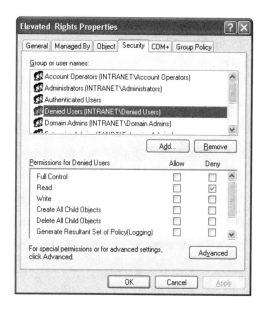

From now on, all the objects you place in this OU will be hidden from all the users that are members of the Denied Users group.

TIP *Be very careful with this operation because in AD, denies always override allow permissions. So even though you (as an administrator) have full rights to this object, all you have to do is be a member of the Denied Users group to lose access to the objects in the OU.*

DC-35: Managing Saved Queries

Activity Frequency: Ad hoc

Active Directory also allows you to create and save queries you use on a regular basis. This means that if you're looking for a series of objects whose selection is complex, you can create the query once, save it, and then reuse it on a regular basis.

All saved queries are stored within the Saved Queries folder within the directory. This folder is located directly below Active Directory Users and Computers in the console of the same name.

To create a saved query:

1. Launch the **Global MMC** (**Quick Launch Area | Global MMC**) and move to **Active Directory Users and Computers** (**Computer Management | Active Directory Users and Computers**).

2. Right-click on **Saved Queries** and select **New | Query**.

3. Type the name of the query (for example, Disabled Accounts) and a description for it. To define the query, click **Define Query**.

4. In the **Define Query** dialog box, select the criterion for your query. For example, if you are looking for all disabled accounts, check **Disabled Accounts** in the Common Queries category. Click **OK**.

5. Click **OK** to save the query.

From now on, all you need to do to locate all the disabled accounts in your directory is to double-click on the **Disabled Accounts** query.

DC-36: Managing Space within AD

Activity Frequency: Ad hoc

Windows Server 2003 now supports the assignation of NTDS quotas—quotas that are assigned to security principals within the Active Directory. These quotas control the number of objects a security principal can create within any given AD partition.

SECURITY SCAN *Assigning NTDS quotas is a good practice because it ensures that no one user or computer account can create enough objects in AD to create a denial of service situation by creating so many objects that the DC will run out of storage space. This situation could also affect network bandwidth as the attacked DC tries to replicate all new data to its peers.*

Quotas affect every object in the directory. For example, if you set general quotas to 1,000, that means that no single AD object can own more than 1,000 other objects. This includes both active objects and tombstone objects—objects that have been removed from the directory, but not yet deleted (because their removal has not been replicated to all partners yet). You can also set a weight to tombstone data. This means that instead of allowing a tombstone object to have the same weight as an active object, you could tell the directory that they take up less space than active objects.

TIP   The default lifetime of tombstone data is 60 days. This is because this data can sometimes be used by AD to help damaged data during a restore operation.

Finally, you can also create groups and assign them different quotas than the general quota. For example, if you want to give print servers the right to own more than 1,000 print queues, you would create a group, include all the print servers in it, and grant it a higher quota. By default, the directory does not contain any quotas.

Quotas can be assigned to every directory partition—configuration, domain, and application—but not the schema partition. The latter cannot hold quotas. For more information on application partitions, see **Procedure DN-04**.

TIP *A quota value of -1 signifies an unlimited quota.*

To set general quotas:

```
dsadd quota partitionname -acct accountname
-qlimit value
```

where *partitionname* is the distinguished name of the partition to which you want to add a quota, *accountname* is the distinguished name of the account (can be a user, group, computer, or InetOrgPerson object), and *value* is the amount of the quota you are adding.

To obtain the names of the partitions in your directory, type:

```
dsquery partition
```

To view a quota limit or verify the results of your previous command, type:

```
dsget quota domainroot -qlimit ">=499"
```

This will list all of the accounts that have a limit greater than or equal to 499.

You should set quotas on all partitions (except the schema, of course). In most organizations, a quota limit of 500 should be appropriate. Remember that you can always create exception quotas.

Quotas should be set for two groups: Domain Users and Domain Computers. This way, you address most of the valid accounts in your domains.

TIP *Quotas are set at the domain level. Be sure to assign quotas in each domain in your forest.*

For example, to set a quota of 500 for the Domain Users group on the TandT.net domain partition, type:

```
dsadd quota dc=TandT,dc=net -acct "cn=Domain
Users,cn=users,dc=TandT,dc=net" -qlimit 500
```

TIP   *The Domain Users distinguished name is in quotes because there is a space in the group's name.*

DC-37: Managing the LDAP Query Policy

✓ Activity Frequency: Ad hoc

By default, Active Directory does not contain an assigned LDAP query policy. This policy controls how LDAP queries will be treated by the directory. At least one policy should be assigned to each domain in your forest.

4

SECURITY SCAN   *Assigning an LDAP query policy is good practice because it protects the directory from denial of service attacks based on LDAP queries. While this is good practice for internal-facing directories, it is an absolute must for any AD that is located in a perimeter or demilitarized network zone.*

Don't worry if you feel you don't know enough about LDAP to define a query policy; AD includes a default query policy that can be used to protect your directory. To assign the default query policy to your directory:

1. Launch the **Global MMC** (**Quick Launch Area | Global MMC**) and move to **Active Directory Sites and Services** (**Computer Management | Active Directory Sites and Services**).

2. Click the name of a domain controller (**Computer Management | Active Directory Sites and Services | Sites |** *sitename* **| Servers |** *DCname*) where *sitename* and *DCname* are the names of the site where the DC is located and the name of the DC you want to view.

3. Right-click on **NTDS Settings** in the details pane and select **Properties**.

4. On the **General** tab, select **Default Query Policy** from the **Query Policy** drop-down list.

5. Click **OK**.

This operation is only required on one DC in the domain.

To modify or create your own query policy, use the `ntdsutil` command in the `LDAP policies` context. Use the Help and Support Center to find more information about this command.

DC-38: Managing the AD Database

Activity Frequency: Ad hoc

Active Directory automatically compacts the NTDS.DIT database on a regular basis, but this compaction does not clear unused space from the database—it only reorganizes data to make it more accessible. Once in a while, you will want to compact the database to clear unused space and reduce its size. The command used to do so is the `ntdsutil` command. The advantage of performing this operation is that it both compacts and defragments the database. In very large AD environments, this can have a significant impact on performance. As such, this operation should be performed on a monthly basis in these environments.

TIP   *Compacting the database must be done offline. This means you must reboot the DC in Directory Services Repair Mode (DSRM) before performing this operation. See* **Procedure DC-29** *for more information.*

Once the DC has been rebooted in Directory Services Repair Mode, and you have logged on with the DSRM administrative password, launch a command console and type:

```
ntdsutil
files
compact to foldername
quit
quit
```

where *foldername* is the name of the destination folder where the compacted database will be stored.

TIP   *In very large directories, this operation may take quite some time.*

Once the operation is complete, take a backup copy of the original database and move the newly compacted database to the original database location.

 **SECURITY SCAN**   *Make sure you protect the original database backup carefully. This database includes a lot of sensitive information.*

Namespace Server Management (DNS)

The Domain Naming Service (DNS) is at the very core of the operation of Active Directory. It supports the logon process and it provides the hierarchical structure of the AD database. As a best practice, you should always marry the domain controller function with the DNS service.

Like all services, the Windows Server DNS includes several tools for management and administration. The first is the DNS console, which is added automatically to the Computer Management console on servers where the service is installed. This DNS console can also be accessed through the Manage Your Server interface. In addition, Windows Server includes the dnscmd command-line tool. Finally, the nslookup and ipconfig commands are useful for DNS updates and problem troubleshooting.

DN-01: DNS Event Log Verification

Activity Frequency: Daily

DNS automatically records its event information in the DNS Log of the Event Viewer. It is recommended that you verify this log daily to ensure the proper operation of your DNS. To verify the DNS Event Log:

1. Launch the Global MMC console and click **Computer Management**.

2. Connect to the appropriate server (**Action | Connect to another computer**) and either type in the server name (\\servername) or use the **Browse** button to locate it. Click **OK** when done.

3. Move to the **DNS Server Event Log** (**System Tools | Event Viewer | DNS Server**).

4. Review the log content for the last day. Take appropriate action if you identify warnings or errors.

You can also enable a temporary trace log directly within DNS. To do so, right-click on the DNS server name (**Computer Management | Services and Applications | DNS | *servername***), move to the **Debug Logging** tab, and enable the **Log packets for debugging** option. You may type in the log filename if you wish, but by default the log file is named DNS.log and is located in the %SystemRoot%\System32\DNS folder. Don't forget to turn off extra logging when you're done, because it puts an additional strain on the DNS server.

DN-02: DNS Configuration Management

Activity Frequency: Monthly

Most organizations will use two DNS infrastructures: an internal infrastructure based on Windows Server and integrated to the production Active Directory, and an external infrastructure that may or may not be based on Windows technologies. The latter depends on when you created your Internet zones and the technological choices you made at the time.

Once thing is certain (or should be): your internal DNS structure will run on Windows Server because you are using Active Directory. Because Windows Server supports automatic addition and removal of DNS records (in conjunction with the DHCP service), all your DNS servers should be set to enable automatic scavenging of stale records (**Computer Management | Services and Applications | DNS | *servername* | Properties | Advanced** tab). This automatically keeps your DNS database clean.

You can perform this activity manually by right-clicking on the server name in the DNS console and selecting **Scavenge Stale Resource Records**. It is also a good idea to **Update Server Data Files** (from the same context menu) on a regular basis. You can also initiate scavenging from the command line:

```
dnscmd servername /startscavenging
```

where *servername* is the name of the server you want to initiate scavenging on. You can also verify the operation of DNS with AD through the `dnslint` command. To verify the DNS operations related to Active Directory:

```
dnslint /ad /s DNSserverIPaddress /v
>filename.txt
```

where you supply the IP address of one of your DNS servers to make sure the `dnslint` command only checks your internal AD-based forest and does not go to the

InterNIC to validate DNS information. The /v switch turns on verbose output. You pipe this command into a text file because its output is significant.

DN-03: DNS Record Management

Activity Frequency: Ad hoc

Even though DNS is dynamic in Windows Server, you will find that you need to add and remove records manually once in a while. To add a DNS record:

1. Launch the Global MMC console and click **Computer Management**.

2. Connect to the appropriate server (**Action | Connect to another computer**) and either type in the server name (\\servername) or use the **Browse** button to locate it. Click **OK** when done.

3. Move to **DNS (Computer Management | Services and Applications | DNS)**. Click the appropriate Forward or Reverse Lookup Zone to load it into the console.

4. Right-click on the zone and select **New recordtype** where *recordtype* is the type of record you want to create.

5. Fill in the appropriate information for the record and click **OK** to create it.

You can also manage records from the command line:

```
dnscmd servername /recordadd zone nodename
recordtype recorddata
```

where *servername* is the server you want to perform the operation on, *zone* and *nodename* is where you want to locate the record in DNS, *recordtype* is the type of record you want to add, and *recorddata* is the information you want to add. You can also use the dnscmd command to enumerate all records on a server:

```
dnscmd servername /enumrecords zone @ >filename.txt
```

Using the @ symbol automatically enumerates all records in the zone root. You pipe this command into a file to capture all output.

DN-04: DNS Application Partition Management

✔ Activity Frequency: Ad hoc

Active Directory stores DNS information in application partitions. These partitions allow you to create a specific replication scope within the directory. For example, by default forest-wide DNS information is contained in a forest-wide partition and domain-centric DNS information is contained only within the actual domain. DNS application partitions are created automatically as you install DNS through DCPromo (**Procedure DC-28**), but you can also create them manually through the context menu of the DNS server in the DNS console.

You can also use the dnscmd command to create additional partitions:

```
dnscmd /CreateBuiltinDirectoryPartitions option
```

where *option* refers to the partition scope and can be either /Domain, /Forest, or /AllDomains. To enumerate existing partitions:

```
dnscmd /EnumDirectoryPartitions
```

TIP   *When creating a multidomain forest, you need to use "dummy" delegations to force the DCPromo Wizard to install DNS and create the domain application partition in the domain itself. If not, DCPromo will create the domain application partition in the forest root domain. You then have to use the dnscmd command to move the partition.*

To create a "dummy" delegation before running DCPromo to create a child domain:

1. Use the Global MMC to connect to the forest root server and move to the parent zone (**Computer**

Management | Services and Applications | DNS |
servername | Forward Lookup Zone | *zonename*).

2. Right-click on the parent zone to select **New Delegation** from the context menu. This launches the New Delegation Wizard. Click **Next**.

3. Type in the **name of the domain** you want to delegate. Click **Next**.

4. Click **Add.** Type in the fully qualified domain name of the first domain controller in the child domain (the name it will have, for example, ChildDomainOne.Intranet.TandT.net) and type in its IP address. Click **Add** and then click **OK**. The server is added to the delegation list. Click **Next**.

5. Click **Finish** to complete the delegation.

TIP *It is important to give the server the FQDN it will have once the child domain is created. This way, DCPromo will try to validate the name during the installation of AD and will be forced to install DNS and create the proper application partition, because the name resolution will not work (the name does not exist until after AD has been installed).*

Chapter 5

Administering Application Servers

So far you've covered a number of different administrative tasks treating both member servers and domain controllers. The final tasks discussed here are focused on sharing applications to support both generic and mission-critical functionalities within your network. Because of this, several server roles are covered in the same chapter. Each plays a part in the application-sharing process.

Administrative Activities

Application servers include servers that either run web-based applications using the .NET Framework or they run more conventional applications whose functionalities are sometimes provided remotely through Windows Terminal Services.

In addition, as an administrator you'll need to monitor the proper operation of all servers, especially to identify if the resources that have been provided for each service meet the demand. Table 5-1 outlines the administrative activities required to ensure proper operation of the application services you deliver to your user community. It also includes activities related to performance management. As always, the frequency of each task is also covered in this table.

Remember to personalize the task list to adapt it to your environment.

Procedure Number	Activity	Frequency
Dedicated Web Servers		
WS-01	Application Event Log Verification	Daily
WS-02	IIS Server Status Verification	Weekly
WS-03	IIS Server Usage Statistic Generation	Monthly
WS-04	Web Server Log Verification	Monthly
WS-05	IIS Security Patch Verification	Ad hoc
WS-06	Web Server Configuration Management	Ad hoc
Applications Server		
AS-01	Shared Application State Verification	Weekly
AS-02	COM+ Application Administration	Weekly
AS-03	.NET Application Administration	Weekly
AS-04	Database Server Administration	Weekly
AS-05	Server Application Client Access	Ad hoc
AS-06	User Software Installation	Ad hoc
Terminal Servers		
TS-01	Terminal Service Connection Management	Weekly
TS-02	Terminal Service Printer Management	Ad hoc
TS-03	Session Directory Management	Ad hoc
TS-04	Terminal Service Licensing Administration	Ad hoc
TS-05	TS User Access Administration	Ad hoc
TS-06	Terminal Service Application Management	Ad hoc
Performance and Monitoring		
PM-01	Router and Firewall Log Verification	Daily
PM-02	General Disk Space Monitoring	Weekly
PM-03	System Resource Management	Weekly
PM-04	Network Traffic Monitoring	Weekly
PM-05	Server Capacity Management	Monthly
PM-06	System Diagnostics	Ad hoc

Table 5-1.   Identity Service Administration Task List

Procedure Number	Activity	Frequency
PM-07	Corporate Error Reporting Management	Ad hoc
PM-08	Monitoring Tools Review	Ad hoc

Table 5-1.   Identity Service Administration Task List *(continued)*

Administration of Dedicated Web Servers

5

Windows Server 2003 introduces a new server role, the blade server or dedicated web server. This role is available through the Web Edition of Windows Server 2003. This edition is a trimmed-down version of the Standard Edition and has limited functionality at certain levels. For example, it cannot support the domain controller role.

Though not all of your web servers will be dedicated, the actions you perform to administer web servers are the same, whether they are dedicated or not. You should, however, consider running dedicated web servers for security reasons: the smaller the service footprint on a server, the better you can protect it.

The activities you will cover here focus mostly on the use of the Internet Information Service (IIS) Manager console and the `iisweb` command-line tool.

TIP *It is a very good idea to download the IIS 6.0 Resource Kit. Search for it at www.microsoft.com/downloads.*

WS-01: Application Event Log Verification

Activity Frequency: **Daily**

IIS sends Active Server Pages (ASP) errors to the Windows Application Event Log. These errors include anything from the launch of web sites to errors when client requests fail.

To view this log, you use the same steps as **Procedure GS-03**, but of course, you do so with the Global MMC console:

1. Launch the **Global MMC** console (**Quick Launch Area | Global MMC**).

2. Connect to the appropriate server, if required (**Action | Connect to another computer**), and either type in the server name (\\servername) or use the **Browse** button to locate it. Click **OK** when done.

3. Move to the **Application Event Log** (**System Tools | Event Viewer | Application**).

4. This log stores all events related to applications. You might want to filter or sort events to view only IIS events. The best way to do so is to click the **Source** button in the header of the details pane. This automatically sorts all errors according to source. Locate IIS events by searching for ASP events.

5. Identify any errors or warnings. Take appropriate action if either appears.

By default, IIS only logs a subset of ASP errors into the Event Log. This subset includes the error numbers 100, 101, 102, 103, 104, 105, 106, 107, 115, 190, 191, 192, 193, 194, 240, 241, and 242.

> *SCRIPT CENTER The Microsoft TechNet Script Center includes a series of WSH sample scripts that helps you perform event log administration tasks. These scripts can be found at http://www.microsoft.com/technet/ treeview/default.asp?url=/technet/scriptcenter/logs/ default.asp?frame=true.*

WS-02: IIS Server Status Verification

Activity Frequency: Weekly

You should also regularly verify the status of your web servers and the web sites they host. This task is set to a weekly frequency, but depending on the criticality of your web server (external presence, company access point, or 24/7 operation), you may decide to do it on a daily basis.

There are two ways to do this. The first involves the Internet Information Services (IIS) Manager console.

TIP *Add the IIS Manager console to the Global MMC using **Procedure GS-17***.

To verify the status of web servers:

1. Launch the **Global MMC** console (**Quick Launch Area ∣ Global MMC**).

2. Connect to the appropriate server if required (**Action ∣ Connect to another computer**) and either type in the server name (\\servername) or use the **Browse** button to locate it. Click **OK** when done.

3. Move to the **IIS Manager** (**Computer Management ∣ IIS Manager**).

4. Verify that each web site is running by right-clicking on it and viewing the status of its service. You can also right-click on the site and select **Browse** from the context menu. The IIS Manager will display the site in the details pane.

5. **Close** or minimize the Global MMC when done.

You can also verify the status of each server and each web site through the command line. This is the second way to verify server status. Use the following command:

```
iisweb /query /s servername
```

where *servername* is the name of the server running the web service. In fact, to automate this process, create a command file, insert a command line for each server, and pipe the results of the entire command file to a text file. Use **Procedure GS-19** to schedule this task to run every week. Then, you only need to check the results in the text file every week.

WS-03: IIS Server Usage Statistic Generation

Activity Frequency: Monthly

One of the activities that you should do on a regular (monthly) basis is the gathering of web server usage statistics. These statistics will help you identify if your servers have the capacity to respond to all requests over time. They will also be useful for the evaluation of peak and off-peak web site usage.

The best way to view web server statistics is to use performance counters. You can create a performance monitoring console that automatically tracks web site usage on all servers. This console will need access rights to performance counters on each server you monitor, so it is best to use the **Run As Shortcut** created in **Procedure GS-01** to launch the **Global MMC Console** (**Quick Launch Area | Global MMC**), and then proceed as follows:

1. Move to **Counter Logs** (**Computer Management | Performance Logs and Alerts**). Right-click in the details pane and select **New Log Settings** from the context menu.

2. The **New Log Settings** dialog box opens. Name your activity log **Web Statistics** and click **OK**.

3. The Web Statistics property page opens. Click **Add Counters**.

4. In the **Select counters from computer** field, type in the name of the server you want to monitor.

5. Select **Web Service** as the performance object and add the following counters using **All instances**:

   • Anonymous Users/sec
   • Current Anonymous Users
   • Nonanonymous Users/sec
   • Current Nonanonymous Users
   • Connection Attempts/sec

6. Repeat the procedure with **Web Service Cache** as the performance object.

TIP *You must monitor both the web service and the web service cache if you want to see the total number of users visiting your sites.*

7. Click **Add** for each counter object. Repeat for each web server and then click **Close**.

8. Set the sampling interval to every **15 seconds**. Then, type in the name of the user you want this activity log to run under. This account needs administrative privileges on each server. It is best to use a domain account to facilitate access. The account should be in the form DOMAIN\accountname. Next click **Password**, type in the password, verify the password, and click **OK**.

9. Move to the **Log Files** tab and select the log file format. **Binary Files** is the default, but log files can also be stored in a SQL Server if it is available. Type in a comment to describe the activity log.

10. Move to the **Schedule** tab. Set the **Start Log** time, and set the **Stop Log** time to after **7 days**. In the **When the log file closes** section, click **Start a new log file**. Click **OK** to close the dialog box.

This will automatically log all web usage activity. To view the results of the activity log:

1. Open the **Performance** console (**Start Menu** | **Administrative Tools** | **Performance**).

2. Under **System Monitor**, click the small database icon in the System Monitor toolbar at the top of the details pane. This is the **View Log Data** button.

3. Select **Log Files** and click **Add**. Locate your log file, click **OK**, and click **OK** to close the **View Log Data** dialog box.

The System Monitor will display the statistics you gathered. You can now view the data in either Graph, Histogram, or Report view.

WS-04: Web Server Log Verification

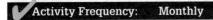

Activity Frequency: Monthly

Besides logging events to the Event Log, IIS logs all events automatically in its own journal. This log is automatically generated by the IIS service. It includes detailed information about each web site. To verify the existence of this log:

1. Launch the **Global MMC** console (**Quick Launch Area | Global MMC**).

2. Connect to the appropriate server if required (**Action | Connect to another computer**) and either type in the server name (\\servername) or use the **Browse** button to locate it. Click **OK** when done.

3. Move to **Web Sites** (**Computer Management | IIS Manager | Web Sites**) and right-click on it to select **Properties** from the context menu.

4. The **General** tab includes the option to **Enable logging**. By default, the Active log format is **W3C Extended Log File Format**. Click **Properties** to view the log configuration.

5. The **Logging Properties** dialog box gives you access to the location of the log under the **General** tab. It also lets you determine the frequency of the log schedule. The **Advanced** tab lets you determine log content (see Figure 5-1). Click **OK** or **Cancel** to close this dialog box. Click **OK** or **Cancel** again to close the **Web Site Properties** dialog box.

Log files are stored under the %SystemRoot%\System32\ LogFiles\W3SVCx folder (where x represents the number of the folder). To view the contents of your log files, move to this folder and double-click on any file.

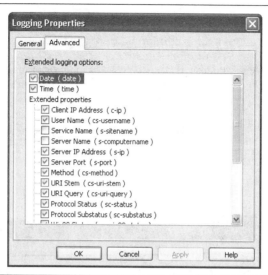

Figure 5-1. The Advanced tab lets you select the information to log.

SECURITY SCAN *It is a good idea to review IIS log files on a regular basis for potential attacks. Look for repeating patterns in the way users visit your site. If your site has authentication enabled, look for repeated attempts to log in from unknown sources.*

TIP *You should use **Procedure FS-02** to make regular backups of your IIS log files. You should also clear the log files after you back them up, to clear up disk space on the IIS server.*

WS-05: IIS Security Patch Verification

Activity Frequency: Ad hoc

IIS has long been a hacker's favorite. This is why you need to pay special attention to security patches for this service.

TIP *This task is set as Ad hoc because you never know when there will be a need to perform it. At minimum, you should perform it on a monthly basis.*

Use **Procedure GS-14** to verify security updates from both the Microsoft web site and other sites such as the SANS Institute. For Microsoft information, go to the Microsoft Hotfix and Security Bulletin Service at http://www.microsoft.com/technet/treeview/default.asp?url=/technet/security/current.asp. Select IIS 6.0 under **Product/Technology** and click **Go**.

Download, test, and install any applicable patches. If you haven't already done so, you should use **Procedure GS-13** to sign up for security bulletin notification.

WS-06: Web Server Configuration Management

Activity Frequency: **Ad hoc**

IIS includes the ability to back up and restore configurations from its metabase, the database that holds all information about the web sites and operational settings for IIS on a server. This tool can be used to generate multiple versions of the same settings from server to server. Thus, if you're running a web farm using the Network Load Balancing service, you can easily generate a single configuration for the front-end web servers, then duplicate it by generating metabase backups.

Make sure your web server configuration is finalized, and then proceed as follows to generate the configuration backup:

1. Launch the **Global MMC** console (**Quick Launch Area | Global MMC**).

2. Connect to the appropriate server if required (**Action | Connect to another computer**) and either type in the server name (\\servername) or use the **Browse** button to locate it. Click **OK** when done.

3. Move to the **IIS Manager** (**Computer Management | IIS Manager**).

4. Right-click on the server name and select **All Tasks | Backup/Restore Configuration**. Click **Create Backup** in the **Configuration Backup/Restore** dialog box.

5. Name the backup and include the date in the name. Click **Encrypt backup using password**, type and confirm the password, and click **OK** to generate the backup. Click **OK** once again to close the dialog box.

Use the same procedure in reverse to restore the configuration settings to the same server. During the restore procedure, IIS will warn you that restoring a metabase is a significant task that modifies all IIS settings on the computer.

TIP   *Restoring an IIS metabase in this manner should only be done on the same server because the backup includes server-specific information that will not run on another server.*

5

To copy a metabase configuration from one server to another, use the `iiscnfg` command. Begin by opening a session on the server from which you want to copy the metabase, and use the following command:

```
iiscnfg /copy /ts targetservername
```

where *targetservername* is the name of the server you want to copy the metabase to. This command automatically removes server-specific information from the metabase settings, letting the configuration settings work on the new server.

TIP   *You must also perform a backup and restore of the contents of each web site to the new server. Make sure the file paths are the same from server to server; otherwise, the metabase configuration settings will not be valid. Use **Procedures FS-02** and **BR-05** to perform this task.*

**SECURITY SCAN**   *You must have administrative rights on both the source and target servers to perform this command. If you are not running in an administrative context, then you must add the* /u username *and* /p password *switches to the command.*

Administration of Application Servers

Conventional application servers run applications in shared mode. In comparison to web servers, the application server is much more of a file server sharing an application folder. Applications are loaded into the server's memory and users make use of the server's capacity to run the shared application.

Because of the nature of conventional application servers, many of the operations used to administer them resemble the operations used to manage file servers.

Application servers also run both COM+ and .NET Framework applications. In addition, they can also host databases and relational database systems. Finally, you need to manage the resources on application servers to ensure they provide adequate performance.

SECURITY SCAN *Microsoft has made considerable changes in the security structure of Windows Server 2003. Because of this, many applications may not run appropriately on this version of Windows. You can download a document titled Guide to Application Compatibility Changes in Windows Server 2003 to review these changes. Search for it at www.microsoft.com/downloads.*

TIP *Microsoft has also produced a Windows Application Compatibility Toolkit. This toolkit is in Version 3.0 and includes information about developing applications for Windows XP/2003 and tools for testing the compatibility of existing applications. It is very useful for system administrators needing to deploy new or legacy applications on Windows Server 2003. Search for it at www.microsoft.com/downloads.*

AS-01: Shared Application State Verification

Activity Frequency: Weekly

You should regularly verify the state of the shared applications you run. There are several ways to do so, but the one you choose depends on the type of application you're running. Take, for example, a shared version of Microsoft Office. The shared version is configured by performing an administrative installation of Office on a server in a file share. Then, you perform a minimal installation on users' computers. Users run the application by launching it on their desktops. The application mostly runs on the server, using the server's processing capacity to perform the operations users need.

But because Office runs in this manner, it is difficult to verify if the application is running properly. You could always go to a computer that has the client components installed and simply launch the application. This will tell you if it is performing properly. You can also use the connectivity tools in Windows Server to view connections to the application's shared folder (see **Procedure FS-03**). This will tell you the number of users currently running the application and the files they currently have open, letting you identify which applications are currently open.

To verify connections and open files:

1. Launch the **Global MMC** console (**Quick Launch Area I Global MMC**).

2. Connect to the appropriate server if required (**Action I Connect to another computer**) and either type in the server name (\\servername) or use the **Browse** button to locate it. Click **OK** when done.

3. Move to the **Sessions** (**Computer Management I System Tools I Shared Folders I Sessions**). View the number of open sessions in the details pane.

5

4. Next, move to **Open Files** (**Computer Management | System Tools | Shared Folders | Open Files**). View the files that are currently in use in the details pane.

5. If you need to close the share or an open file, you can right-click on the share or the file in the details pane and select **Close Session** or **Close Open File** from the context menu in each respective item.

TIP *You should send a message to users if you are going to close either a session or a file. Use the* net send *command to do so. Type* **net send /?** *for more information.*

You can also view open sessions and open files through the command line:

```
net session servername
net file
```

where *servername* is the NetBIOS name of the server in \\servername format.

TIP *The* net file *command cannot be executed remotely. You must be on the server itself to use this command.*

AS-02: COM+ Application Administration

Activity Frequency: Weekly

COM+ application administration is greatly facilitated in Windows Server 2003. This version of Windows offers several powerful management features for the operation of COM+ applications:

- **Applications as NT Services** All COM+ applications can be configured as NT Services, making applications load at boot time or on demand as required.

- **Low-Memory Activation Gates** Windows Server can check memory allocations before it starts a process, allowing it to shut an application down if it will exhaust memory resources. This allows other applications running on the server to continue operation, while only the faulty application fails.

- **Web Services** Any COM+ object can be treated as a web service and any web service can be treated as a COM+ object, greatly extending the remoting capabilities of your applications.

- **Application Partitions** In terms of application support, these partitions allow you to host several instances of the same or different versions of COM+ objects on the same server. If, for example, you have 500 customers running a hosted application, you can create 500 partitions, one for each customer— segregating their operational environment from all of the others. They also control the replication scope within a domain.

- **Application Recycling** Some applications have a tendency to have degraded performance over time due to memory leaks and other programmatic issues. Windows Server can recycle a process by gracefully shutting it down and restarting it on a regular basis. This can be done either administratively or through the COM+ software development kit. Administratively, it is applied through the **Component Services** console by right-clicking on a COM+ component, selecting **Properties**, and modifying the elements on the **Pooling & Recycling** tab. By default, all COM+ applications use recycling.

Verifying the state of COM+ applications focuses on using the Component Services portion of the Global MMC to verify if COM+ components are running or not. You can also use the new COM+ features of Windows Server to add resilience to your COM+ applications.

 **SECURITY SCAN** *Be wary of modifying security settings on COM+ components. One wrong move and the application will not work anymore, and you'll have a very hard time trying to find the problem.*

To run an application as a service:

1. Launch the **Global MMC** console (**Quick Launch Area | Global MMC**).

2. Move to **Computers** in **Component Services** (**Computer Management | Component Services | Computers**).

3. Connect to the appropriate server if required (**Action | New | Computer**) and either type in the server name (\\servername) or use the **Browse** button to locate it. Click **OK** when done.

4. Locate the COM+ component you want to run as a service and right-click on it to select **Properties** from the context menu.

5. Move to the **Activation** tab and click **Run as NT Service**. Windows Server will warn you that it may reset some settings; click **OK**. Next, click **Setup new service**.

6. In the **Service Setup** dialog box, choose the **Startup Type**, set the **Error Handling** level, and identify **Dependencies**. Click **Create** to set up the service.

7. Click **OK** to close the **Properties** dialog box.

To enable and manage application partitions in Active Directory, first enable partitions on the server:

1. Launch the **Global MMC** console (**Quick Launch Area | Global MMC**).

2. Move to **Computers** in **Component Services** (**Computer Management | Component Services | Computers**).

3. Connect to the appropriate server if required (**Action | New | Computer**) and either type in the server name (\\servername) or use the **Browse** button to locate it. Click **OK** when done.

4. Locate the server for which you want to enable partitions and right-click on it to select **Properties** from the context menu.

5. Move to the **Options** tab and check **Enable Partitions**. You can also enable **Check local store when choosing partition for user**, but do so only if you want the server to locally store partitions as well as within AD. Click **OK**.

6. Next, move to the **AD Users and Computers** portion of the Global MMC. Enable **Advanced Features** (**View | Advanced Features**).

7. Create partitions in the **ComPartitions** container (**Computer Management | AD Users & Computers | System | ComPartitions**) and create partition sets or groups of partitions under **ComPartitionSets**. Partition sets are used to assign partition access to users and groups.

8. Once partitions are created in AD, return to **Component Services** portion of the **Global MMC** (**Computer Management | Component Services**), locate the computer you want to include in the partition, and right-click on **COM+ Partitions** to select **New | Partition**. This launches the **New Partition Wizard**.

9. Click **Next**. Determine the partition type. It can be a previously exported partition or it can be an empty partition. If your development team has prepared the partition previously, select the first option; otherwise, select **Create an empty partition**. Click **Browse Directory** to find the partition you created in AD, select the partition, and click **Add**. Click **Next**, then **Finish**.

10. Finally, you can protect the partition against deletion by right-clicking on it and selecting **Properties**. Click **Disable deletion** in the **Advanced** tab. Click **OK** when done.

Application partition users should be assigned in AD so that they are available domain wide.

> **SCRIPT CENTER** *The Microsoft TechNet Script Center includes a sample script that helps you identify COM+ Partition Sets. This script can be found at http://www.microsoft.com/technet/treeview/default.asp?url=/technet/ScriptCenter/user/ScrUG125.asp?frame=true.*

AS-03: .NET Application Administration

Activity Frequency: Weekly

Since Windows Server includes a built-in version of the .NET Framework (Version 1.1), it makes it easy for any corporation to make use of the .NET Framework to build and run applications. Administrators need to verify that .NET Framework applications are running properly and that their security access rights are properly configured. In fact, administrators need to perform the following tasks when managing .NET Framework applications:

- **Manage the assembly cache** This involves the administration of assemblies that are shared by several applications.

- **Manage configured assemblies** This involves the administration of assemblies from the assembly cache that have defined rule sets.

- **Configure code access security policy (CASP)** This defines the rule sets for assembly access permissions.

- **Adjust remoting services** This involves the administration of communication channels for the applications running on a server. By default, both the HTTP and the TCP clients are allowed communication channels.

- **Manage individual applications** This involves the administration of special properties for specific applications.

- **Manage patches and upgrades** This involves verifying the Microsoft download web site (www.microsoft.com/downloads) for patches and upgrades to the .NET Framework. (Just search for the .NET Framework on the download site.)

The administration of .NET applications is performed either through the .NET Framework Configuration Console or the .NET Framework Wizards. Both are found within Administrative Tools (**Start Menu | Administrative Tools**). The wizards include three tools that walk you through a configuration process: Adjust .NET Security, Trust an Assembly, and Fix an Application.

In actual fact, it is easiest to perform administrative tasks through the console since you have already added this snap-in to the Global MMC in **Procedure GS-17**. As you will see, this snap-in gives you a lot of assistance through the details pane.

The most important activity is the management of code access security policies. This can be done through two of the wizards or through the console. The wizards only work for two policies: the machine and user policies. Policies are always applied in the same order: enterprise, machine, and user. You can set a default level of policy for the Common Language Runtime (CLR) to apply by telling the .NET Framework to stop policy application at a specific level. For example, if you consider that your enterprise policy is secure enough, you can tell the CLR to stop policy processing at the enterprise level. This will cause the CLR to ignore both the machine and the user policies.

When you browse through the default policies in the .NET Framework Configuration console (**Global MMC | Computer Management | .NET Configuration 1.1 | My Computer | Runtime Security Policy**), you will see that the default set of policies is quite extensive. Right-clicking on the objects listed in the console tree will give you access to their properties. CLR security is quite granular and can be applied at several levels.

A code access permission set can include permissions for all levels of the .NET Framework. This includes everything from local access to the file system to access to the registry. You can create your own permission sets. For example, you might determine that you prefer a higher level of trust for applications originating from within your intranet. The best way to determine what works best for your environment is to try them out. Begin with the default security policies and refine them as you become more familiar with the .NET Framework. The most important recommendation for use of the .NET Framework is to migrate all code to managed code.

Once you've refined the policy set for your applications, you can use the .NET Configuration 1.1 console (go to **Runtime Security Policy | Create Deployment Package**) to generate a Windows Installer package (.msi) that will capture your configuration changes and allow you to deploy them to other application servers using **Procedure DC-15**.

AS-04: Database Server Administration

Activity Frequency: Weekly

Windows Server 2003 is the ideal database server because it has the ability to manage processes intelligently. SQL Server 2000 has been optimized to run on this platform, but Windows Server will also support other databases that run on Windows. While there is no default database within Windows Server, it is still important to mention here that one of your system administration tasks for application servers involves database administration. At the very least, it means you need to verify the status of the server, its memory availability, and the proper operation of its disks.

Use **Procedure GS-02** to verify the status of your database services. Use **Procedure FS-01** or **PM-02** to verify the status of the disks running the database system. And use **Procedure PM-05** to verify the status of RAM on your database servers.

SCRIPT CENTER The Microsoft TechNet Script Center includes a sample script that helps you connect to an ADO database. This script can be found at http://www.microsoft.com/technet/treeview/default.asp?url=/technet/scriptcenter/entscr/ScrEnt03.asp?frame=true.

AS-05: Server Application Client Access

✔ Activity Frequency: Ad hoc

Granting access to conventional applications is performed in much the same way as granting access to file shares. In fact, since the application resides on a file share and that file share access is managed through groups (usually global groups), granting or denying access to an application can be as simple as inserting or removing a user account from the appropriate group. Use **Procedure FS-03** to grant group access to new shared applications and use **Procedure DC-05** to add or remove users from the appropriate security group.

5

However, some shared applications require the delivery of a portion of code on the desktop to be able to run. This is the case for Microsoft Office, for example. Use **Procedure AS-06** to define the installation for each desktop and then use **Procedure DC-15** to deliver it to the right desktops.

AS-06: User Software Installation

✔ Activity Frequency: Ad hoc

All software in your network should be integrated to the Windows Installer service. If this is the case, you can perform administrative installations of the MSIs you use to allow users to run server-based applications rather than locally installed applications. Administrative installations have a lot of advantages over locally installed applications.

First, they allow administrators to better control the way an MSI package installs, especially giving administrators the ability to include transforms to customize the package installation. When users install the minimal version from the administrative install, they do not need to reapply the transform—only perform a normal installation. Second, administrative installations are fully fault tolerant. Third, administrative installations are easier to patch because they only need to be patched on servers. Fourth, if your products need activation (like Microsoft Office), they only need to be activated in one place. Fifth, administrative installations tend to have a smaller footprint than desktop installations.

TIP *Once the administrative point has been created, do not change the disk structure where the installation is stored because computers record where the installation originated from in their Windows Installer "source list." Plan a server/disk infrastructure around storing packages and stick to it.*

To perform an administrative installation of an MSI package on a server:

1. On the server, type the following command:

```
msiexec /a package.msi
```

where *package.msi* is the name of the software package you want to install. Windows Installer will display a dialog box requesting the network location for the installation. Either type in the name of the folder or click the **Browse** button to locate it.

2. Click **Next**. Windows Installer will display the **Admin Verify Ready** dialog box. Click **Next**. Click **Finish** when the installation is complete.

TIP *If you need to transform the installation to customize it, use the following command:*
```
msiexec /a package.msi adminproperties =
"transforms=transform.mst"
```
This will embed the transform into the administrative installation to automatically deliver it upon client installation.

Now you can perform client installations from the administrative installation:

On the client, type the following command:

```
msiexec /i \\servername\sharename\package.msi /qn
```

where *servername**sharename**package.msi* is the name and the network share path of the software package you want to install and the /i and /qn switches, respectively, mean install and quiet with no user interaction. Windows Installer will automatically install the package in quiet mode.

You can use **Procedure DC-15** to deploy the administrative installation to user systems.

TIP *If you perform this installation on a domain-based distributed file share, you will automatically build in fault tolerance for the administrative installation because Windows Installer will automatically link up to either the closest or any available server. You can use **Procedure FS-06** to do so.*

5

SCRIPT CENTER *The Microsoft TechNet Script Center includes sample scripts that help you install software on a local or remote computer. These scripts can be found at http://www.microsoft.com/technet/treeview/ default.asp?url=/technet/scriptcenter/compmgmt/ScrCM2 8.asp?frame=true and http://www.microsoft.com/technet/ treeview/default.asp?url=/technet/scriptcenter/compmgm t/scrcm29.asp?frame=true.*

Administration of Terminal Services

One of the greatest features of Windows Server 2003 is the Terminal Services (TS) server. This service enables you to publish applications to remote computers, giving them full access to programs running on the Windows Server environment. The greatest advantage is in deployment. Since the application operates on the terminal server, it is the only place it needs to be installed, updated, and maintained. Unlike conventional shared applications, no client component is required other than the Remote Desktop Connection (RDC) agent. Besides the RDC client, you only need to deploy a shortcut to users, and this shortcut doesn't change even though you may upgrade or otherwise modify the application.

> **TIP** *If clients are running Windows XP, they already have the RDC client.*

Terminal Services supports sound redirection to client PCs; thus, if you operate a multimedia application on the server, users will hear the information just as if the application were running on their own workstation. In addition, the Windows Server version of Terminal Services supports higher-quality graphics, including True Color and the highest level of resolution supported by client hardware. Resolution and color must be set on both the client and the server to operate. Finally, TS is now integrated with Group Policy, allowing you to control Terminal Service features centrally.

Thin-client models are becoming more and more popular, especially with the proliferation of wireless Pocket PCs and the new Tablet PC device. Both have more limited resources, making server application hosting more and more attractive to these user bases.

> **TIP** *Not all applications are terminal server "aware." Be sure to verify the support an application has for Terminal Services before acquiring it.*

The tools you use to work with Terminal Services include:

- The Group Policy Management Console to centrally control TS GPOs
- Terminal Services Manager to configure TS connections
- Command-line tools for session and user management

> **TIP** *Microsoft provides two good documents for terminal service setup and preparation. The first is a document on terminal service security settings called "Locking Down Windows Server 2003 Terminal Server Sessions." The second is a document outlining how to size terminal servers called "Windows Server 2003 Terminal Server Capacity and Scaling." Both can be found at www.microsoft.com/downloads.*

TS-01: Terminal Service Connection Management

✔ Activity Frequency: Weekly

You should verify TS connections at least on a weekly basis. The best tool to use is the Terminal Services Manager. Unfortunately, this console cannot be added to the Global MMC.

5

TIP *To obtain full functionality from the Terminal Services Manager console, you must first connect to a TS server remotely, and then launch the console on the server. This places you within the TS environment and gives you access to such features as remote control and connection creations.*

To verify TS connections:

1. Launch the **Global MMC** console (**Quick Launch Area | Global MMC**).

2. Move to **Remote Desktops** (**Computer Management | Remote Desktops**) and click the connection name for a TS server. This opens an RDC connection to the server.

3. On the TS server, launch the **Terminal Services Manager** (**Start Menu | Administrative Tools | Terminal Services Manager**).

TIP *It is a good idea to place this tool in the Quick Launch Area for every TS server.*

4. Click the server name in the left pane to view current connections. Click the domain name in the left pane to view connections on other servers in your domain.

5. Review the status of each connection.

You can use the TS Manager to perform administrative activities. For example, if you want to view a session in progress or assist a user, you right-click on the user's connection and select Remote Control. This will launch a window, letting you view the user's actions on the server.

You can also review connections through the command line. To identify all TS servers in your domain:

```
query termserver
```

This command lists all terminal servers in your domain. If there exists more than a single page, it pauses at each new page.

To view the connections on a TS server:

```
query session /server:servername /counter
```

where *servername* is the DNS name of the server. Using the `/counter` switch also displays the information about the current TS counters, including number of sessions created and terminated. You can also pipe the results of this query into a text file and schedule the task using **Procedure GS-19** on a weekly basis. This allows you to verify connection status simply by reviewing the results in the text file.

SCRIPT CENTER *The Microsoft TechNet Script Center includes a sample script that helps you read information about TS sessions. This script can be found at http://www.microsoft.com/technet/treeview/default.asp?url=/technet/ScriptCenter/user/ScrUG143.asp?frame=true.*

TS-02: Terminal Service Printer Management

Activity Frequency: Ad hoc

Through the configuration of Group Policies for Terminal Services, printers may be automatically created when users connect to a Terminal Services session. When users disconnect from a session, even if sometimes they do not always use the proper method, these printers are automatically deleted from the terminal server. But special conditions must be met for these printers to be created.

First, your GPO must define client printing settings. Terminal Service printing settings are found in **Computer Configuration** | **Administrative Templates** | **Windows Components** | **Terminal Services** | **Client/Server Data**

Redirection. By default, Terminal Services allows printer redirection and LPT port redirection, and automatically sets the client's default printer as the default printer for the TS session. If you want to specify these settings explicitly, use **Procedure DC-16** to apply these settings to a GPO that affects all TS users.

Second, the terminal server must have all local printer drivers installed. If a user has a local printer connection and the terminal server does not have the printer driver installed, TS does not create the connection. You must inventory all printers and install proper printer drivers on your TS servers. Use **Procedure PS-03** to install drivers on the server.

TS-03: Session Directory Management

Activity Frequency: Ad hoc

Terminal servers can provide automatic load balancing through the combination of two features: the Network Load Balancing (NLB) service and the Session Directory. This creates a Terminal Services cluster. When users are connected to a terminal server, and they disconnect but don't close their session, they are automatically reconnected to the same session through the Session Directory the next time they activate a TS session.

Session directories are created through a series of services. First, you must enable the NLB service. Use **Procedures NC-01** and **NC-02** to set up the NLB service for terminal servers.

Next, ensure the Session Directory settings are enabled in Group Policy. These settings are found under **Computer Configuration I Administrative Template I Windows Component I Terminal Services I Session Directory**. The settings required are:

- Terminal Server IP Address Redirection
- Join Session Directory
- Session Directory Server
- Session Directory Cluster Name

The last two settings must include both the Session Directory server name and the cluster name. Use **Procedure DC-16** to apply the GPO. Make sure it is a GPO that is applied to all terminal servers.

You must also make sure that all the terminal servers that participate in the cluster are contained within each server's Session Directory computer's local group. The best way to do this is to create a global group that contains all of the computer accounts for the terminal servers, and then insert this group into each server's Session Directory computer's local group. Then, if you need to add a new server to the group, you can use **Procedure DC-05** to add the server's computer account to the global group.

TS-04: TS Licensing Administration

Activity Frequency: **Ad hoc**

Unlicensed terminal servers will only allow clients to operate for 120 days, after which all sessions will end and the terminal server will no longer respond to client requests. In order to license servers, you must install a terminal server license server. This server must be activated by Microsoft before it can begin to issue licenses to your enterprise. Activation is automatic if your server is connected to the Internet.

Once the server is activated, you can add new Client License Key (CLK) packs as your TS client population grows. These packs must be purchased from Microsoft before they can be added to your network.

To add a new CLK pack:

1. Launch the **Terminal Services Licensing** console (**Start Menu | Administrative Tools | Terminal Services Licensing**).

2. Right-click on the server name and select **Install Licenses** from the context menu. This starts the **Terminal Server CAL Installation Wizard**.

3. Enter the appropriate licensing information in **Program and Client License Information** and then click **Next**.

4. The wizard then connects to the Microsoft Clearing House and installs the license key packs. Click **Finish** when done.

TS-05: TS User Access Administration

Activity Frequency: Ad hoc

By default, terminal servers issue licenses to any computer that requests one. You must enable the **License Server Security Group** GPO setting (**Computer Configuration |
Administrative Templates | Windows Components | Terminal Services | Licensing**) to restrict TS sessions to authorized groups of computers or users only. Use **Procedure DC-16** to do so, and make sure this policy is applied to all TS servers.

Once this is done, you will need to create global groups for users (or computers) that are allowed to use Terminal Services and place these groups within the local **Terminal Services Computers** group that is created by the policy. Then, you can use **Procedure DC-05** to add or remove users from the global group and thus enable or disable their access to your terminal servers.

TS-06: TS Application Management

Activity Frequency: Ad hoc

Terminal Services applications should be installed through Add or Remove Programs, because this component ensures that applications are installed in multiuser mode. Multiuser mode is a requirement for all applications that are shared through Terminal Services.

To install a new application on a terminal server:

1. Use the Global MMC to open a **Remote Desktop Connection** to the appropriate server (**Computer Management | Remote Connections**) and launch the **Windows Explorer (Quick Launch Area | Windows Explorer**).

2. Expand **My Computer** and click **Control Panel**.

3. Double-click on **Add or Remove Programs** and click **Add New Programs**.

4. If the program is published in Active Directory and is available in the program list, select it and click **Install**. If not, click **CD or Floppy**. This launches the **Install Program Wizard**.

5. If your program is on CD, insert it and click **Next**. If your program is on a network drive, click **Next**. The wizard will search both floppy and CD drives for the program. When it doesn't find it, it will let you browse for the location of the application. You can either type in the path and name of the installation file or click **Browse** to locate it. Click **Next**.

6. Click **Finish** to install the application.

Applications can also be installed through the command line. To install applications from the command line:

```
change user /install
```

This sets the terminal server in installation mode. Perform the installation. Then type the following command:

```
change user /execute
```

This resets the terminal server into execution mode.

---

*TIP The Terminal Services application operation model is slightly different from the standard Windows model because of the multiuser environment. You should always check for compatibility scripts for the applications you install. These scripts modify standard installations to make them TS compatible. They should be run after the application installation. Scripts are found in the %**SystemRoot%\ Application Compatibility Scripts\Install** folder.*

Performance and Monitoring Administration

The last activity category that administrators must plan for in their busy schedule is performance and monitoring. This means evaluating if the technologies you have in place perform well, if their capacity is adequate to the task, and if they require fine-tuning or additional components. It also includes the verification and monitoring of critical systems to ensure that they are operating properly. Several tools can be used for this activity. Two are especially useful:

- The Performance Console, which includes the System Monitor

- The Network Monitor

A third tool can be downloaded from the Microsoft web site. It is the Windows System Resource Manager. This tool is, in fact, a portion of the Microsoft Operations Manager that has been made available for administrators of Windows Server 2003 to monitor and manage system resources.

SCRIPT CENTER   The Microsoft TechNet Script Center includes a series of sample scripts that helps you monitor Windows Server systems. These scripts can be found at http://www.microsoft.com/technet/treeview/ default.asp?url=/technet/scriptcenter/monitor/default.asp ?frame=true.

PM-01: Router and Firewall Log Verification

Activity Frequency: Daily

Monitoring activities include the verification of log files from all sources. Routers and firewalls are not necessarily based on Windows Server 2003, though this operating system can perform both tasks. In fact, Windows Server's routing capabilities rival those of complex routers such as Cisco or Nortel. Windows Server routers even support open shortest path first (OSPF) routing.

Windows Server also includes the Internet Connection Firewall (ICF), a stateful firewall that can help protect computers that are exposed to the Internet from unauthorized access. ICF is especially useful when used in conjunction with Windows Server's Internet Connection Sharing (ICS) feature.

TIP *Many networks do not rely on Windows Server for either routing or firewall protection. Rather, they rely on specialized hardware to perform these tasks. If this is the case in your network, you should still verify both logs on a weekly basis.*

Both the firewall and the routing features of Windows Server support activity logging. The routing feature mostly uses the system event log for activity logging. When used in conjunction with the Internet Authentication Service (IAS), it also logs information in IAS format. You can use **Procedures GS-03** and **RV-02** to check the appropriate logs on a weekly basis.

To view logging information for the ICF, you should first make sure logging is enabled on the network card performing the ICF service. This is done through the network connection's Property data sheet:

1. Use the Global MMC to open a **Remote Desktop Connection** to the appropriate server (**Computer Management | Remote Connections**) and launch the **Windows Explorer (Quick Launch Area | Windows Explorer**).

2. Move to the **Control Panel** and select **Network Connections** in the left pane. In the details pane, right-click on the network connection running the ICF service and select **Properties** from the context menu.

3. Move to the **Advanced** tab and click the **Settings** button.

4. Move to the **Security Logging** tab. Select **Log Dropped Packets** and if you want complete logging information, then also select **Log Successful Connections**. Note the path and name of the logging file: %SystemRoot%\ pfirewall.log. Click **OK**.

5. Click **OK** to close the network connection Property sheet.

From now on, you can verify the firewall log by examining the %SystemRoot%\pfirewall.log file. Make a habit of archiving this file on a weekly basis. The firewall log will automatically overwrite entries in this log when it has reached its size limit (4MB).

When you verify either the routing or the firewall logs, look for unusual patterns in the log entries. This will help you identify suspect behavior.

PM-02: General Disk Space Monitoring

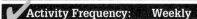
Activity Frequency: **Weekly**

In **Procedure FS-01**, you verify free disk space for data disks on file servers. It is also good practice to perform the same verification on all the disks of your servers. You can use the same procedure to perform this verification. The best way to do so is to create a performance monitor that is geared to disk space. This console will need access rights to performance counters on each server you monitor, so it is best to use the **Run As Shortcut** created in **Procedure GS-01** to launch the **Performance Monitoring Console** (**Start Menu I Administrative Tools I Performance**), and then proceed as follows:

1. Use the plus symbol (+) in the toolbar to add a counter.

2. In the **Select counters from computer** field, type in the name of the server you want to view.

3. Select **LogicalDisk** as the performance object and **% Free Space** as the counter.

4. Make sure you select all disk drive(s) and click **Add**, and then **Close**.

5. When all the servers and disks are added, use **File | Save As** to place the console under your **My Documents** folder and name it **All Disk Monitor.msc**. Use this console to view free space on all your servers from now on.

You should check this console on a weekly basis.

TIP *If more automated solutions are needed, Microsoft Operations Manager (MOM) Can Be Used To Provide proactive alerting on disk space issues. More information is available at http://www.microsoft.com/mom/.*

PM-03: System Resource Management

✓ Activity Frequency: **Weekly**

The Enterprise and DataCenter editions of Windows Server 2003 include an additional tool for system resource management. It is the Windows System Resource Manager (WSRM). This tool can be found on retail versions of the installation CDs for both editions.

TIP *The Windows System Resource Manager can also be found at http://www.microsoft.com/windowsserver2003/ downloads/wsrm.mspx. This download is an ISO image and must be burned to CD-ROM before it can be installed.*

The WSRM can be used in two manners. First, it can be used to profile applications. This means that it helps you identify how many resources an application requires on a regular basis. When operating in this mode, WSRM only logs events in the application event log when the application exceeds its allowed limits. This helps you fine-tune application requirements.

The second mode offered by the WSRM is the manage mode. In this mode, WSRM uses its allocation policies to control how many resources applications can use on a server. If applications exceed their resource allocations, WSRM can even stop the application from executing.

WSRM also supports alerts and event monitoring, much the same way as Microsoft Operations Manager can. It is a powerful tool that is designed to help you control CPU, disk, and memory usage on large multiprocessing servers.

By default, the WSRM includes two management policies: the default policy, which simply reports on application use, and the Equal per User policy, which allocates resources equally based on the number of users connected to an application.

Operating the WSRM is very similar to operating the Performance console—you determine what to manage by adding and removing counters for specific objects. Finally, the WSRM supports application auditing, letting you know how and when applications are used on your servers.

Use the WRSM to first evaluate how your applications are being used, then apply management policies. Make sure you thoroughly test out your policies before applying them in your production environment. You can use **Procedure DC-05** to create special security groups that can be used as pilots for your new management policies. This way, you will be able to get a feel for the WSRM before you fully implement it in your network.

When you're ready, you can use the Calendar to determine when which policy should be applied (see Figure 5-2).

TIP *If you are managing several servers with the WSRM, you may need to dedicate resources to it since it is resource intensive. You might consider placing it on a dedicated management server if this is the case.*

PM-04: Network Traffic Monitoring

Activity Frequency: Weekly

Like previous versions of Windows, Windows Server 2003 includes the Network Monitor, a tool that allows you to capture network packets and view the content of the traffic on your networks. This tool is not installed by default.

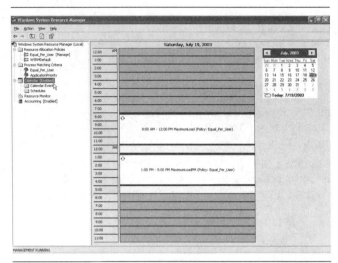

Figure 5-2. The WSRM Calendar lets you assign different policies at different times.

It must be added through the Add or Remove Programs interface in the Control Panel. Since it is a Windows component, you need to select **Add/Remove Windows Components**. Once the **Windows Components** dialog box is open, select **Management and Monitoring Tools** and then click **Details** to select **Network Monitor Tools**. Click **OK**, and then **Next** to perform the installation. The Windows Server installation CD is required for this installation.

Once the Network Monitor is installed, it can be accessed through Administrative Tools (**Start Menu | Administrative Tools**). Since you intend to use this tool on a weekly basis, you should place it in your Quick Launch Area.

 *Network Monitor can be installed on either servers or workstations. It is preferable to install this tool on a workstation to secure and limit its use. To further protect it, use **Procedure GS-01** to create a Run As shortcut to launch Network Monitor.*

To view traffic on your network:

1. Launch the **Network Monitor** and provide appropriate credentials for its use.

2. Choose the network interface to monitor. By default, Network Monitor selects the local network interface.

3. Click the **Start** button on the toolbar to begin capturing packets (see Figure 5-3).

4. Click **Stop and View Traffic** when you have captured enough data.

5. In the View Traffic pane, examine the data provided by the traffic on your network. **Close** the View Traffic pane to return to the Network Monitor. **Save** the capture so that you can perform future comparisons. **Close** the Network Monitor when done.

Look for unusual patterns to identify unauthorized behavior on your network. This task should be done weekly, but you may decide to perform it at different times to get a more complete picture of the traffic patterns on your network.

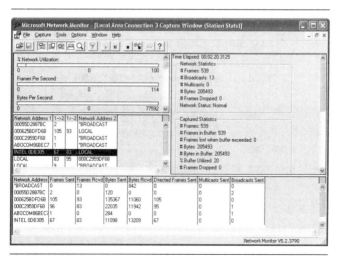

Figure 5-3. The Network Monitor lets you track network traffic.

PM-05: Server Capacity Management

✔ Activity Frequency: Monthly

Server capacity management should be reviewed on a monthly basis. The best tool for viewing server capacity is the Performance console. It allows you to capture data on how your servers perform on a regular basis.

TIP *You should also use this procedure every time you stage a new server, to create an original baseline for the server. This way, you can compare results to the original baseline and determine how the workload is changing as well as what you need to modify on the server to maintain performance levels.*

You can use **Procedure PM-02** to create a special server capacity monitoring console that will track the following elements for each server in your network:

- Free disk space (% free physical disk space and % free logical disk space)
- Disk usage time (% physical disk time and % logical disk time)
- Disk reads and writes (physical disk reads per second and physical disk writes per second)
- Disk queuing (average disk queue length)—*active by default*
- Memory usage (available memory bytes)
- Memory paging (memory pages per second)—*active by default*
- Paging file activity (% paging file usage)
- Processor usage (% processor time)—*active by default*
- Interrupts (processor interrupts per second)
- Multiple processor usage (system processor queue length)
- Server service (total server bytes per second)
- Server work items (server work item shortages)

- Server work queues (server work queue length)
- Server paged pool (server pool paged peak)

Use the **Explain** button in System Monitor to learn what each setting refers to. Monitor these settings over time to identify how your servers perform. Once you are confident that you know how your servers should perform, set or adjust your service level agreements based on this performance. Then, if you see long-term performance deviations (compared to the original baseline), you can increase server capacity through its growth mechanisms.

5

PM-06: System Diagnostics

Activity Frequency: Ad hoc

Once in a while, you will need to perform system diagnostics on a server to help identify recurring problems. So far, you've used several procedures to help examine items like the event logs and review how servers perform on an ongoing basis. But, when you do identify problems, you sometimes need to get more information about the troublesome system. One good tool for this job is the **System Information** console (**Start Menu | All Programs | Accessory | System Tools | System Information**).

This console provides information about the hardware resources, components, software environment, and Internet settings on any server in your network. To view information from another server, click **Remote Computer** (**View | Remote Computer**) and type in the name of the server you want to view. You can also use it to view **System History** (**View | System History**), letting you identify changes to your systems over time.

The System Information console is actually part of the Windows Help and Support Center (H&SC). It also gives you access to four other tools that provide additional information on your system. These include:

- Network Diagnostics, which scans your system to identify the status of networking components

- File Signature Verification Utility, which lets you identify which drivers are signed and which are not—and can thus potentially destabilize your system

- DirectX Diagnostics Tool, which provides information about multimedia components on your server

- Dr. Watson, which helps provide diagnostics about application problems

In addition, it includes a powerful search utility for quick information location (see Figure 5-4).

Use the System Information console to help you identify problematic situations on your servers.

TIP   *Microsoft Product Support has made several of its own reporting tools available. These tools can analyze and report on the directory service, server clusters, Microsoft Data Access Components (MDAC), network performance, SQL Server and Software Update Services. To obtain them, search for the Microsoft Product Support Reporting Tools at www.microsoft.com/downloads.*

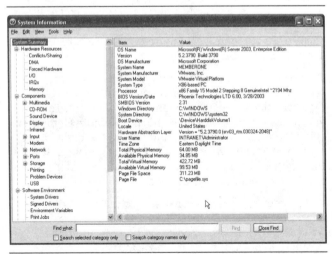

Figure 5-4.   The System Information console tells you about system status.

PM-07: Corporate Error Reporting Management

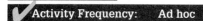

Activity Frequency: Ad hoc

Since Windows XP and Office XP, all Microsoft applications are designed to automatically generate error reports. In fact, they use Dr. Watson to generate error reports and send them to Microsoft.

You can, however, contain error reporting internally through the use of Group Policy Objects. Corporate Error Reporting GPOs are located in **Computer Configuration | Administrative Templates | System | Error Reporting**. To control error reporting internally, use **Procedure DC-16** to apply the following GPO settings to all systems:

- Under **Computer Configuration | Administrative Templates | System | Error Reporting:**

- Enable the **Report Errors** setting. Check **Do not display links to any Microsoft provided "more information" Web site** as well as **Force queue mode for application errors**. Type in the file upload path to a server share in UNC format and type in the words to use to replace the words "Microsoft" in all error reports.

- You might also disable **Display Error Notification**. Since your **Error Reporting** setting is enabled, if you enable this setting, users will have to decide whether or not to report the error. If you are testing new applications, you most likely will want all errors reported. This is why you should disable this setting.

- Under **Computer Configuration | Administrative Templates | System | Error Reporting | Advanced Error Reporting Settings,** you can configure how error reporting will behave and which types of errors it should send.

Additionally, Microsoft has released a tool for the examination and analysis of corporate error reports. This tool is contained within the Microsoft Office XP Resource Kit and can be found at the Microsoft download web site. Search for Corporate Error Reporting at www.microsoft .com/downloads. The Office Resource Kit tool set is 11MB in size, but you will want to install only the corporate error reporting analyzer. To do so, select **Custom Installation** and deselect all other Resource Kit tools from the installation menu. Once installed, you can use the **Edit** menu to modify the **Default Policy** to gather reports from your internal file server.

PM-08: Monitoring Tools Review

Activity Frequency: Ad hoc

Once or twice a year, you should take the time to review the toolkit you use to monitor performance on your network. Are the tools you use acceptable? Do they perform adequately? Do they provide you with the information you require to properly manage resources in your environment?

If any of the above questions is answered in the negative, you should take the time to review the various products on the market that focus on monitoring activities. One good tool for network monitoring and performance management is the Windows System Resource Manager's big brother, Microsoft Operations Manager. MOM includes several "management packs" that allow you to monitor special server roles. More information on MOM can be found at http://www.microsoft.com/mom/.

Final Notes

This book provides over 160 different tasks that administrators should perform on a regular basis to properly manage their Windows Server networks. Its goal is to help simplify the workload administrators everywhere must undertake to ensure their network properly delivers services to their user communities.

If you find that some tasks have not been covered, or if you find new and innovative ways to perform the tasks listed here, feel free to share them with us. We, in turn, will place them on the companion web site to help further enhance the administration experience for Windows Server networks.

You can contact us at PocketAdmin@Reso-Net.com. Don't forget to visit the companion web site at www.Reso-Net .com/PocketAdmin.

5

Appendix A

Task Frequency List

Use the following table to plan the frequency of your administrative activities. Refer to the table of contents for the location of each task description.

Procedure Number	Activity	Frequency
BR-01	System State Backup Generation	Daily
BR-02	Backup Verification	Daily
CS-01	Clusters: Cluster State Verification	Daily
CS-02	Clusters: Print Queue Status Verification	Daily
DC-01	User Management	Daily
DC-02	User Password Reset	Daily
DC-03	Directory Service Log Event Verification	Daily
DC-04	Account Management	Daily
DC-05	Security Group Management	Daily
DN-01	DNS Event Log Verification	Daily
FS-01	Available Free Space Verification	Daily
FS-02	Data Backup Management	Daily
FS-03	Shared Folder Management	Daily
FS-04	File Replication Service Event Log Verification	Daily
GS-01	Run As Shortcuts	Daily
GS-02	General Service Status Verification	Daily
GS-03	System Event Log Verification	Daily
GS-04	Security Event Log Verification	Daily
GS-05	Service and Admin Account Management	Daily
GS-06	Activity Log Maintenance	Daily
PM-01	Router and Firewall Log Verification	Daily
PS-01	Print Queue Management	Daily

Procedure Number	Activity	Frequency
WS-01	Application Event Log Verification	Daily
AS-01	Shared Application State Verification	Weekly
AS-02	COM+ Application Administration	Weekly
AS-03	.NET Application Administration	Weekly
AS-04	Database Server Administration	Weekly
BR-03	Off-site Storage Tape Management	Weekly
CS-03	Clusters: Server Cluster Management	Weekly
CS-04	Clusters: Quorum State Verification	Weekly
DC-06	KCC Service Status Management	Weekly
DC-07	AD Replication Topology Verification	Weekly
DC-08	Global Catalog Status Verification	Weekly
DC-09	Universal Administration Group Management	Weekly
DC-10	Account Policy Verification	Weekly
DC-11	PKI Service Verification	Weekly
DW-01	DHCP Server State Verification	Weekly
FS-05	Volume Shadow Copy Management	Weekly
FS-06	Distributed File System Management	Weekly
FS-07	Quota Management	Weekly
FS-08	Indexing Service Management	Weekly
FS-09	Data Disk Integrity Verification	Weekly
FS-10	Data Disk Defragmentation	Weekly
FS-11	File Access Audit Log Verification	Weekly
FS-12	Temporary File Cleanup	Weekly
FS-13	Security Parameter Verification	Weekly
FS-14	Encrypted Folder Management	Weekly
GS-07	Uptime Report Management	Weekly
GS-08	Script Management	Weekly
GS-09	Script Certification Management	Weekly
GS-10	Antivirus Definition Update	Weekly
GS-11	Server Reboot	Weekly
HW-01	Network Hardware Checkup	Weekly

Procedure Number	Activity	Frequency
NC-01	NLB Cluster State Verification	Weekly
PM-02	General Disk Space Monitoring	Weekly
PM-03	System Resource Management	Weekly
PM-04	Network Traffic Monitoring	Weekly
PS-02	Printer Access Management	Weekly
PS-03	Printer Driver Management	Weekly
RV-01	Remote Access Server Status Verification	Weekly
RV-02	RADIUS/IAS Server State Verification	Weekly
RV-03	Wireless Monitoring	Weekly
TS-01	Terminal Service Connection Management	Weekly
WS-02	IIS Server Status Verification	Weekly
BR-04	Disaster Recovery Strategy Testing	Monthly
BR-05	Restore Procedure Testing	Monthly
BR-06	Backup Strategy Review	Monthly
DC-12	AD Service/Admin Account Verification	Monthly
DC-13	Lost and Found Object Management	Monthly
DN-02	DNS Configuration Management	Monthly
DW-02	WINS Server State Verification	Monthly
FS-15	Data Archiving	Monthly
FS-16	File Replication Service Management	Monthly
GS-12	Security Policy Review/Update	Monthly
GS-13	Security Patch Verification	Monthly
GS-14	Service Pack/Hot Fix Update	Monthly
GS-15	New Software Evaluation	Monthly
GS-16	Inventory Management	Monthly
HW-02	Server BIOS Management	Monthly
HW-03	Firmware and Server Management Software Update Management	Monthly
PM-05	Server Capacity Management	Monthly

A

Procedure Number	Activity	Frequency
RA-01	Server RDC Management	Monthly
RA-02	PC RDC Management	Monthly
RI-01	RIS Server State Verification	Monthly
RV-04	Remote Access Policy Verification	Monthly
WS-03	IIS Server Usage Statistic Generation	Monthly
WS-04	Web Server Log Verification	Monthly
AS-05	Server Application Client Access	Ad hoc
AS-06	User Software Installation	Ad hoc
BR-07	Server Rebuild	Ad hoc
DC-14	Right Delegation Management	Ad hoc
DC-15	Software Installation Management	Ad hoc
DC-16	GPO Management	Ad hoc
DC-17	Computer Object Management	Ad hoc
DC-18	Distribution Group Management	Ad hoc
DC-19	AD Forest Management	Ad hoc
DC-20	AD Information Management	Ad hoc
DC-21	Schema Management	Ad hoc
DC-22	Schema Access Management	Ad hoc
DC-23	Schema Content Modification	Ad hoc
DC-24	Schema-Modifying Software Evaluation	Ad hoc
DC-25	Operations Master Role Management	Ad hoc
DC-26	Operations Master Role Transfer	Ad hoc
DC-27	Operations Master Disaster Recovery	Ad hoc
DC-28	Domain Controller Promotion	Ad hoc
DC-29	Domain Controller Disaster Recovery	Ad hoc
DC-30	Trust Management	Ad hoc
DC-31	Forest/Domain/OU Structure Management	Ad hoc
DC-32	Active Directory Script Management	Ad hoc
DC-33	Forest Time Service Management	Ad hoc
DC-34	Access Control List Management	Ad hoc

Procedure Number	Activity	Frequency
DC-35	Managing Saved Queries	Ad hoc
DC-36	Managing Space within AD	Ad hoc
DC-37	Managing the LDAP Query Policy	Ad hoc
DC-38	Managing the AD Database	Ad hoc
DN-03	DNS Record Management	Ad hoc
DN-04	DNS Application Partition Management	Ad hoc
DW-03	WINS Record Management	Ad hoc
DW-04	DHCP Attribute Management	Ad hoc
DW-05	DHCP Scope Management	Ad hoc
DW-06	DHCP Reservation Management	Ad hoc
DW-07	DHCP Superscope Management	Ad hoc
DW-08	DHCP Multicast Scope Management	Ad hoc
DW-09	DHCP Option Class Management	Ad hoc
DW-10	DHCP/RIS Server Authorization	Ad hoc
FS-17	Disk and Volume Management	Ad hoc
GS-17	Global MMC Creation	Ad hoc
GS-18	Automatic Antivirus Signature Reception	Ad hoc
GS-19	Scheduled Task Generation/Verification	Ad hoc
GS-20	Security Template Creation/Modification	Ad hoc
GS-21	Reference Help File Management	Ad hoc
GS-22	Server Staging	Ad Hoc
GS-23	Administrative Add-on Tool Setup	Ad Hoc
GS-24	Default User Profile Update	Ad Hoc
GS-25	Technical Environment Review	Ad hoc
GS-26	System and Network Documentation	Ad hoc
GS-27	Service Level Agreement Management	Ad hoc
GS-28	Troubleshooting Priority Management	Ad hoc
GS-29	Workload Review	Ad hoc

A

Procedure Number	Activity	Frequency
HW-04	Device Management	Ad hoc
NC-02	NLB Cluster Member Management	Ad hoc
PM-06	System Diagnostics	Ad hoc
PM-07	Coporate Error Reporting Management	Ad hoc
PM-08	Monitoring Tools Review	Ad hoc
PS-04	Printer Sharing	Ad hoc
PS-05	Print Spooler Drive Management	Ad hoc
PS-06	Printer Location Tracking Management	Ad hoc
PS-07	Massive Printer Management	Ad hoc
PS-08	New Printer Model Evaluation	Ad hoc
RA-03	User Support through Remote Assistance	Ad hoc
RA-04	Remote Desktop Connection Shortcut and Web Access	Ad hoc
RI-02	RIS Image Management	Ad hoc
RV-05	NAT Service Management	Ad hoc
RV-06	VPN Connection Management	Ad hoc
TS-02	Terminal Service Printer Management	Ad hoc
TS-03	Session Directory Management	Ad hoc
TS-04	Terminal Service Licensing Administration	Ad hoc
TS-05	TS User Access Administration	Ad hoc
TS-06	Terminal Service Application Management	Ad hoc
WS-05	IIS Security Patch Verification	Ad hoc
WS-06	Web Server Configuration Management	Ad hoc

INDEX

INTERNATIONAL CONTACT INFORMATION

AUSTRALIA
McGraw-Hill Book Company
Australia Pty. Ltd.
TEL +61-2-9900-1800
FAX +61-2-9878-8881
http://www.mcgraw-hill.com.au
books-it_sydney@mcgraw-hill.com

CANADA
McGraw-Hill Ryerson Ltd.
TEL +905-430-5000
FAX +905-430-5020
http://www.mcgraw-hill.ca

GREECE, MIDDLE EAST, & AFRICA
(Excluding South Africa)
McGraw-Hill Hellas
TEL +30-210-6560-990
TEL +30-210-6560-993
TEL +30-210-6560-994
FAX +30-210-6545-525

MEXICO (Also serving Latin America)
McGraw-Hill Interamericana Editores
S.A. de C.V.
TEL +525-1500-5108
FAX +525-117-1589
http://www.mcgraw-hill.com.mx
carlos_ruiz@mcgraw-hill.com

SINGAPORE (Serving Asia)
McGraw-Hill Book Company
TEL +65-6863-1580
FAX +65-6862-3354
http://www.mcgraw-hill.com.sg
mghasia@mcgraw-hill.com

SOUTH AFRICA
McGraw-Hill South Africa
TEL +27-11-622-7512
FAX +27-11-622-9045
robyn_swanepoel@mcgraw-hill.com

SPAIN
McGraw-Hill/
Interamericana de España, S.A.U.
TEL +34-91-180-3000
FAX +34-91-372-8513
http://www.mcgraw-hill.es
professional@mcgraw-hill.es

UNITED KINGDOM, NORTHERN,
EASTERN, & CENTRAL EUROPE
McGraw-Hill Education Europe
TEL +44-1-628-502500
FAX +44-1-628-770224
http://www.mcgraw-hill.co.uk
emea_queries@mcgraw-hill.com

ALL OTHER INQUIRIES Contact:
McGraw-Hill/Osborne
TEL +1-510-420-7700
FAX +1-510-420-7703
http://www.osborne.com
omg_international@mcgraw-hill.com